EDUCATIONAL FACILITIES

THE AMERICAN INSTITUTE OF ARCHITECTS
EXEMPLARY LEARNING ENVIRONMENT PROGRAM

EDUCATIONAL FACILITIES

First published in Australia in 2002 by
The Images Publishing Group Pty Ltd
ACN 059 734 431
6 Bastow Place, Mulgrave, Victoria 3170, Australia
Telephone (+61 3) 9561 5544 Facsimile (+61 3) 9561 4860
email: books@images.com.au
website: www.imagespublishinggroup.com

National Library of Australia Cataloguing-in-Publication Data
Educational facilities: the American Institute of
Architects Exemplary Learning Environment Program.

Includes index.

ISBN 1 86470 098 X.

1. School buildings – United States – Design and
construction. 2. School facilities – United States –
Design and construction. I. American Institute of
Architects.

371.9045

Designed by The Graphic Image Studio Pty Ltd
Mulgrave, Australia

Film by Allardice Graphic Arts Pty Ltd, Australia
Printed by Sing Cheong Printing Company Limited, Hong Kong

IMAGES has included on its website a page for special notices in relation to this and
our other publications. It includes updates to the information printed in our books.
Please visit this site: www.imagespublishinggroup.com

CONTENTS

TWO-YEAR TECHNICAL OR COMMUNITY COLLEGES   190

For many years the AIA's Committee on Architecture for Education (CAE) has produced state-of-the-art slide programs that highlight innovative projects and trends in school design. Now it has launched the Design Awards and Exemplary Learning Environment Program.

The program includes this book and the accompanying CD-ROM, that was released in late 2000. Throughout the book you will find information on a variety of learning environments, from early childhood to community colleges. The overall program is designed to help educators, architects, and planners understand the 14 special criteria needed to produce effective learning environments.

Innovative teaching and learning methods, coupled with increased interest in educational environments, prompted the CAE to revisit its traditional school design recognition programs. Building on its tradition of presenting state-of-the-art programs that highlight innovative projects and trends in school design, CAE is moving to encompass a broader definition of learning environments.

This program marks the beginning of a new type of recognition of exemplary school designs. A five-person jury comprised of a world-renowned architect, a U.S.-based award-winning architect, an educational facility planner, a professor who specializes in educational issues impacting school programming and facility design, and a client, selected the most innovative learning environments that have been designed or planned for the new millennium. Immediately following their deliberations, the jury participated in a roundtable discussion, fielding questions and presenting issues that influenced their selections. This discussion, held at AIA National, was open to CAE members and invited guests.

In addition to recognizing licensed architects in the award process, the CAE also had a special 'Unique Learning Environment Category.' This was open to academics, graduate students, nonprofits, or individuals whose aim it is to design or generate new thinking in learning environments, but who are not architects or do not work in the for-profit sector. Six winners in the category were recognized as such and are part of this program.

This book presents the 24 award winners, including five honor awards, six merit awards, and 11 citations. It also includes examples and ideas from the 77 other projects selected by the jury out of 172 submissions from the U.S. and Canada.

Requirements

All entries had to meet the following requirements:

Educational facilities that were eligible for consideration included domestic as well as international designs for:

- Early childhood learning environments (including Head Start)

- Public, private, and parochial elementary, middle/junior high, and high schools

- Alternative schools (i.e., charter schools, magnet schools, vocational/technical schools, and at-risk schools)

- Innovative learning centers (such as museum schools, environmental learning centers, and high-tech learning environments)

- Two-year technical and community colleges, and corporate or other specialized training centers

Projects included new construction, additions, and renovations. Master plans, including multiple sites and/or multiple phases, were also considered.

Entries were limited to projects that have been completed since 1 January 1995. If the project had not yet been built, it must have been completed through design development, with the owner's approval, to proceed-with-construction documents by 1 June 1999.

Individual designers, educational planners, academics, and nonprofits other than architects were eligible to submit in the Unique Learning Environment category and were highly encouraged to participate. In all other categories, only projects designed by architects licensed in North America were eligible.

Projects were not accepted from firms affiliated with a jury member.

Jury Members

To ensure the quality of the program, the jury reviewed all entries. It had sole discretion in selecting entries that best represent a nationwide cross-section of state-of-the-art educational facilities, early childhood learning environments, K–1 2 schools, innovative learning centers, and two-year technical and community colleges. Honor awards, merit awards, citations, and other special recognition of outstanding features of individual projects were awarded at the jury's discretion.

The jury consisted of the following individuals:

Bruce A. Jilk, AIA, *CAE advisory group, Afton, Minneapolis (Chair)*

Herman Hertzberger, *Architectuur Studio Herman Hertzberger, Amsterdam, The Netherlands*

Carol Ross Barney, FAIA, *Ross Barney+Jankowski Architects, Chicago*

Steven Bingler, AIA, *Concordia Architects, New Orleans*

George H. Copa, PhD, *professor of education, Oregon State University-Corvallis*

Arnie Glassberg, *assistant superintendent, business services, San Lorenzo Unified School District, San Lorenzo, California*

Criteria

The goal of this program was to illustrate current state-of-the-art design in learning environments for children through college-aged adults. Its emphasis was not only on the quality of the physical environment, but also on the comprehensiveness and inclusiveness of the planning process. It was the aim of this program to show how the planning and design process together can translate into an environment that will make a difference in the way students of all ages learn.

One of the first important steps to define an effective learning environment was to determine the necessary and desired criteria. To develop a common understanding and to bridge international perspectives, CAE looked to the Organization for Economic Cooperation and Development (OECD) Programme on Educational Building (PEB) in Paris, France. CAE utilized the criteria from OECD/PEB's publication Schools for Today and Tomorrow.

During the jury deliberation, the members confirmed the importance of the OECD/PEB criteria, but added two others: 'Place of Learning' and 'Creative Materials.' It also combined 'Urban' and 'Rural Contributions' into one item. An additional category was created to reflect the importance of the 'Planning Process' in several entries. This resulted in the 15 categories used to organize these projects. One of the observations the jury made early in their deliberation was the importance of ideas over the importance of projects as a whole. Therefore, each project is assigned to a primary category.

Special jury criteria included:

- Quality design reflecting innovative programs
- Sensitivity to the surrounding context (environmentally and culturally)
- Effective contribution to local urban and/or rural issues
- Imaginative use of site
- Consideration of maintenance costs
- Energy efficiency
- Unique and effective use of space
- Imaginative re-use of existing buildings
- Creative use of materials and building systems
- Innovative design for learning technology
- Support of life-long learning
- Symbiosis with community
- Creative partnership with business and industry
- Location or the Place of Learning

Awards Categories and Special Recognition

The highest honor awards were given to registered architects whose projects represented extraordinary quality design. Merit and citation awards were given to other registered architects for superior quality projects. The balance of the projects are included in this book because of their special recognition in the design of learning environments.

Bruce A. Jilk
Reykjavik, 2001

EDUCATIONAL FACILITIES

EARLY CHILDHOOD LEARNING ENVIRONMENTS

KING URBAN LIFE CENTER AND KING CENTER CHARTER SCHOOL

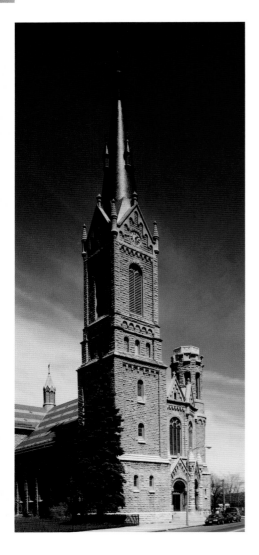

ARCHITECT'S STATEMENT

This facility represents the fusion of a profoundly unique and experimental inner-city early childhood school (pre-K-4) with advanced computer technology connecting it to a larger educational network. It offers support for multiple inner-city program needs for all ages, and involved the resurrection and restoration of a major landmark and community church.

Lead by a small visionary group of dedicated educators and preservationists over a period of 12 years, the program was developed with representatives of the neighborhood community, the local primary public education institution, two colleges, and two universities. The group

ran a pilot program for three years in a nearby public school to develop its teaching and electronic portfolio techniques before design of this facility commenced.

The physical design provides open classrooms with a variety of adjacent multi-use spaces shared by the school and 11 community programs. All classrooms are equipped with iMac computers and video cameras connected through a teleconferencing center to a city-wide network of educational sites. A literacy center/library is planned for the existing choir loft.

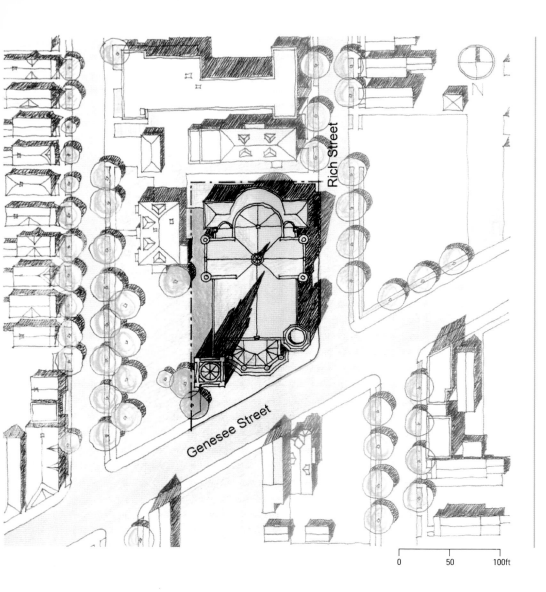

ARCHITECT
Hamilton Houston Lownie
Architects, PC

TYPE OF FACILITY
Early Childhood Learning
Environment / Innovative
Learning Environment / Unique
Learning Environment / Charter
School

TYPE OF CONSTRUCTION
Adaptive Reuse and Restoration

SITE AREA
.53 acres

BUILDING AREA
15,347 square feet

TOTAL PROJECT COST
$2,089,000

STATUS OF PROJECT
Completed 1998

NUMBER OF STUDENTS
90–100

STRUCTURAL ENGINEER
Siracuse Engineers

MECHANICAL/ELECTRICAL ENGINEER
Robson & Woese, Inc.

CONTRACTOR
All State Development Inc.;
H.B. Plumbing; D.V. Brown
Mechanical; Goodwin Electric

THE ALTHEA GIBSON EARLY CHILDHOOD EDUCATION ACADEMY

MERIT

EAST ORANGE, NEW JERSEY

ARCHITECT'S STATEMENT

Increasing evidence links early learning experiences to success throughout school, so the East Orange School District of East Orange, New Jersey, is developing neighborhood early childhood education centers to serve children as young as three years old. The Althea Gibson Early Childhood Education Academy is the first of these centers.

Planning and design was a collaboration involving educators, parents, neighbors, and community organizations. The consensus was to provide a stable, secure environment for young children—something often missing from their home lives. The school was designed to provide a 'main street,' multipurpose room, and shared storytelling areas within a cheerful, multicolored structure. In order to meet the requirements of its funding program, the project was completed in less than 15 months.

The Althea Gibson Early Childhood Education Academy has proved to be a great success, enhancing the community's sense of renewal and optimism about the future of its children.

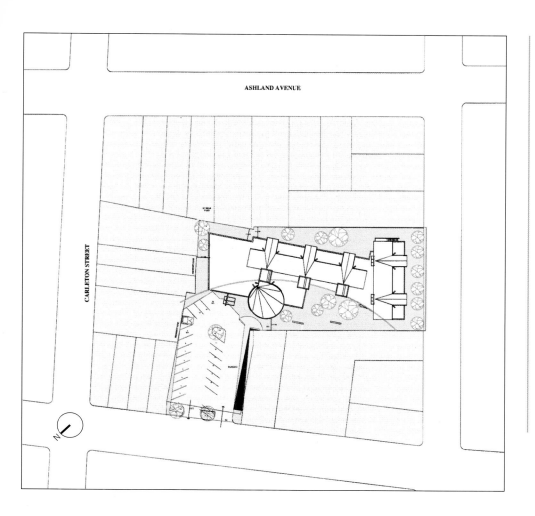

ARCHITECT
Hillier

TYPE OF FACILITY
Early Childhood Learning Environment

TYPE OF CONSTRUCTION
New

SITE AREA
1.25 acres

BUILDING AREA
22,500 square feet

TOTAL PROJECT COST
$5,434,817

STATUS OF PROJECT
Completed 1999

NUMBER OF STUDENTS
180

STRUCTURAL/MECHANICAL/ELECTRICAL ENGINEER
Hillier Engineering & Technology

CONTRACTOR
Christa Construction Inc.

EARLY CHILDHOOD LEARNING ENVIRONMENTS

Day Care Inc.

Architect's statement

A community needed to provide an early childhood learning environment in a farming community on the Delmarva Peninsula. While searching for a location for a new building, a partnership between Day Care Inc. and the school district was developed to provide a learning environment for a wider range of people.

Located adjacent to an elementary school is a four-room, 1936 historic high school constructed as the only secondary school for blacks in the county. It was determined that if the early childhood learning center was located in an expansion area of this structure, then the income would assist in the development of the high school into a museum and place for community learning. Having close proximity, this facility is being used for before- and after-school learning activities for the students of the elementary school. The grouping of these facilities makes for a wonderful partnership between private and public sectors to fill the educational needs of the young and old.

The design of the addition creates a balanced expression of historical and regional elements, and touch of childhood adventure.

ARCHITECT
**Bignell Watkins Hasser
Architects, P.A.**

TYPE OF FACILITY
**Early Childhood Learning
Environment**

TYPE OF CONSTRUCTION
Addition/Renovation

SITE AREA
1.6 acres

BUILDING AREA
7,525 square feet

TOTAL PROJECT COST
$435,582

STATUS OF PROJECT
Completed May 1996

NUMBER OF STUDENTS
143

STRUCTURAL ENGINEER
McCormac Engineering

MECHANICAL ENGINEER
**Siegel, Rutherford, Bradstock &
Ridgway**

CONTRACTOR
Willow Construction, Inc.

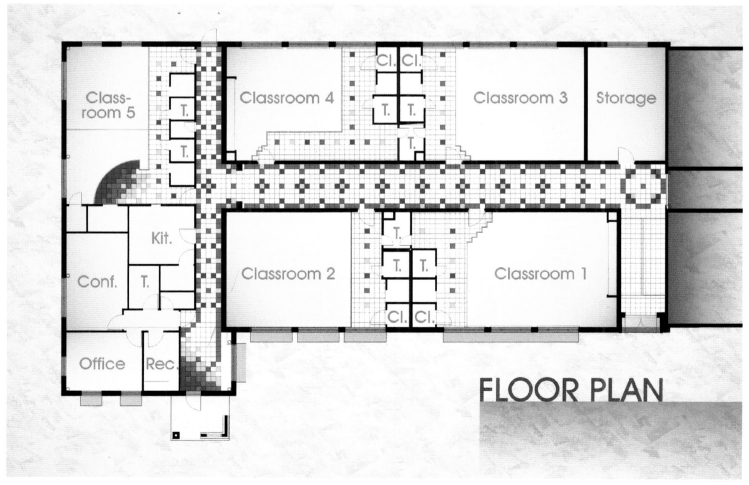

FLOOR PLAN

DONALD A. QUARLES ELEMENTARY SCHOOL

ARCHITECT'S STATEMENT

The process began with a series of brainstorming sessions held with school administration and staff. The primary needs were quickly identified:

- 4–10 additional classrooms
- Integrated computer technology
- Learning environments appropriate to pre-K, kindergarten, and first grade students
- Flexible space for large and small group instruction
- Self-contained classrooms with direct access to individual outdoor playspace.

Design reviews were held with administration, staff, and parents at key milestones throughout project development. Out of this interactive process, the concept for a children's educational village evolved, with self-contained, four-classroom buildings and support facilities linked together by outdoor walkways and play spaces. The playful building forms and materials, the integration of daylight, furniture, and color selection evolved out of an ongoing dialogue with the users.

The design process extended over a year and a half, while the size of the project and the number of required classrooms remained in flux. Based on informal post-occupancy evaluations conducted on site and the enthusiasm of the children, it is readily apparent that the project works.

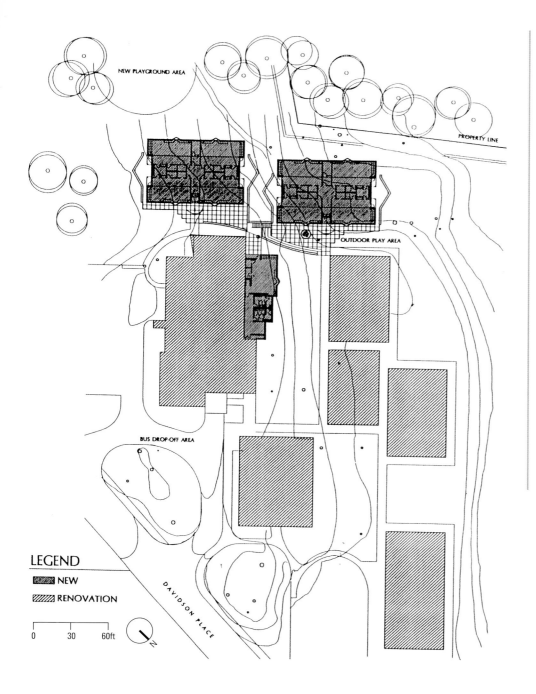

NEW PLAYGROUND AREA

PROPERTY LINE

OUTDOOR PLAY AREA

BUS DROP-OFF AREA

DAVIDSON PLACE

LEGEND

▨ NEW

▨ RENOVATION

0   30   60ft

N

ARCHITECT
EI Associates, Architects & Engineers

TYPE OF FACILITY
Early Childhood Learning Environment / Elementary School

TYPE OF CONSTRUCTION
New/Addition/Renovation

NUMBER OF STUDENTS
225

SITE AREA
9 acres

BUILDING AREA
15,200 square feet

TOTAL PROJECT COST
$3,120,600

STATUS OF PROJECT
Completed September 1997

STRUCTURAL/MECHANICAL/ELECTRICAL ENGINEER
EI Associates, Architects & Engineers

CONTRACTOR
Maharan Construction

EARLY EDUCATION CENTER

EAST BOSTON, MASSACHUSETTS

ARCHITECT'S STATEMENT

Intended to enrich and nurture Boston's very youngest learners, and make their initial school experience positive, this compact, 12-classroom school features playful, childlike colors, shapes, and patterns. The transition between home and the school environment is minimized by placing just two pairs of classrooms per floor, creating more intimate surroundings scaled to the young users. Tables, chairs, counters, windows, sinks, and bathrooms are all child height. Corridors are shorter and narrower; the library, with its low bookcases and tables, feels more like a story nook; the cafeteria is compact; and the multipurpose room features low benches and windows along one wall, bringing the large room down to scale. Also, city-mandated wood floors and traditional wood windows in the classrooms add an appropriate 'homeyness' to this small school.

The site, selected by the city for this new 300-student school, was an already cramped 3.1 acre parcel occupied by a 650-student elementary school and its existing parking and play areas. The new building, placed as close to the street as possible, occupies less than one-third of the total site, leaving a generous playground, which also serves as a neighborhood park, on the sunny corner between the two schools.

The simple block masonry and detailed brick skin mirror the rhythm and scale of the surrounding residential streetscape of brick townhouses, and the bas relief panels along the façade continue a transportation theme established by the neighboring school. The school, designed to reflect its surrounding context while squeezing in behind existing utility poles and street signs, appears to have always been on the site.

3

ARCHITECT
HMFH Architects, Inc.

TYPE OF FACILITY
Early Childhood Learning Environment

TYPE OF CONSTRUCTION
New

SITE AREA
1 acre

BUILDING AREA
36,500

TOTAL PROJECT COST
$8,013,000

STATUS OF PROJECT
Completed September 1998

NUMBER OF STUDENTS
300

STRUCTURAL ENGINEER
Foley & Buhl Engineering, Inc.

ELECTRICAL ENGINEER
TMP Consulting Engineers, Inc.

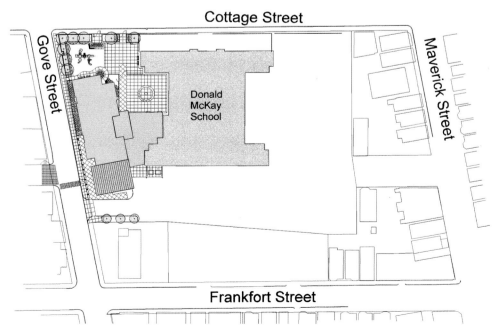

Cottage Street

Gove Street

Maverick Street

Donald McKay School

Frankfort Street

FRANCIS CHILD DEVELOPMENT INSTITUTE, PENN VALLEY COMMUNITY COLLEGE

KANSAS CITY, MISSOURI

ARCHITECT'S STATEMENT

The site utilized a portion of a highly visible, green-space buffer that surrounds the Penn Valley Community College campus buildings. The task: design an addition for a multistory wing of an inwardly focused campus that complements the strong architectural composition of a 1970's master-planned building while providing an inviting public presence.

'Movement' was utilized to create a contrast against the rigid campus architecture while engaging the rolling site. Two primary arcs enclose space, frame views, and provide a gentle approach to the building. The convex façade projects

the institute's offices toward the public to be visible and welcoming. The concave façade sweeps toward the heart of the facility and creates an enclosure for the child development classrooms. The intersection of the arcs defines the entrance, and the intersections of other site walls define outdoor play areas while providing privacy and security.

A series of in-depth design workshops with all team members was critical; these included everyone from the president of the community college, to faculty and staff, to representatives of the private foundation funding the project.

ARCHITECT
Gould Evans Affiliates

TYPE OF FACILITY
**Early Childhood Learning
Environment / Two-year
Technical or Community College**

TYPE OF CONSTRUCTION
Addition/Renovation

SITE AREA
10 acres

BUILDING AREA
35,882 square feet

TOTAL PROJECT COST
$4,848,885

STATUS OF PROJECT
Completed August 1998

NUMBER OF STUDENTS
7,000/152

STRUCTURAL ENGINEER
Bob D. Campbell & Company

MECHANICAL ENGINEER
Henthorn-Sandmeyer & Company

CONTRACTOR
Titan Construction Organization

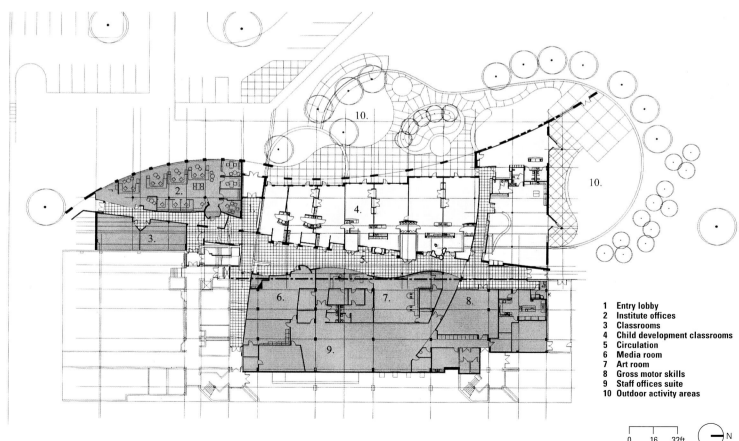

1 Entry lobby
2 Institute offices
3 Classrooms
4 Child development classrooms
5 Circulation
6 Media room
7 Art room
8 Gross motor skills
9 Staff offices suite
10 Outdoor activity areas

0   16   32ft   N

GRETCHKO ELEMENTARY SCHOOL

WEST BLOOMFIELD, MICHIGAN

ARCHITECT'S STATEMENT

This new elementary school is specifically designed for children in pre-school through first grade. Splashed with touches of primary colors, all aspects of the school were crafted to meet the social, physical, and learning needs of the four to six-year-old user. Special attention was given to creating environments 'just for kids' with special windows (at their level) and a symbolic stair platform at the main entry for imaginative play activities.

Floor patterns, French doors, two-level door handles, and access to protected outdoor play areas all add to the spirit of adventure at the school. The facility includes 12 generously sized flexible class areas, a dedicated art and music area, gross motor activity center, and a centrally located media center.

Site development includes separate bus and auto drop-off loops all leading to the 'front door' denoted by the yellow arched graphic. It truly is a facility full of life and happiness!

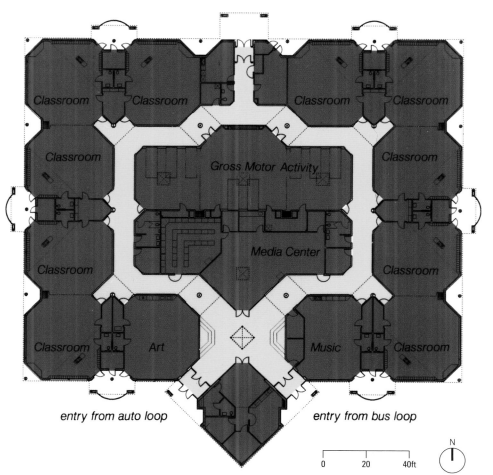

entry from auto loop · entry from bus loop

0 20 40ft

N

ARCHITECT
TMP Associates, Inc.

TYPE OF FACILITY
Early Childhood Learning Environment / Elementary School

TYPE OF CONSTRUCTION
New

SITE AREA
9.1 acres

BUILDING AREA
32,500 square feet

TOTAL PROJECT COST
$4,185,382

STATUS OF PROJECT
Completed August 1995

NUMBER OF STUDENTS
300

STRUCTURAL/MECHANICAL/ELECTRICAL ENGINEER
TMP Associates, Inc.

CONTRACTOR
The Bell Company

SHORELINE EARLY EDUCATION CENTER

WHITEHALL, MICHIGAN

ARCHITECT'S STATEMENT

Programming and design was a joint effort of administrators, teachers, community members, and design team. The focus was centered on developing teaching methodology, establishing program requirements, participative design charrettes, and approving the final scope.

The primary needs unveiled a plan to facilitate the transition of traditional teaching methods to grade level teaming. Teachers not ready to participate in full teaming would have classrooms allowing for more traditional methods—teachers ready to participate would have learning environments to foster all aspects of teaching teams.

The relatively large size of the facility was intimidating—hence, grade level pods allowing each teaching team to center their time in 'neighborhoods' reducing the impact of the building size.

Additional requirements included provisions for learning reinforcement space by creating a flexible environment to support the curriculum delivery. Hands-on learning labs supported this requirement, permitting indoor activity space and group gathering areas for special productions. The shape of the K–1 wing differs from the 2–3 wing—reflecting the more physical nature of the space oriented largely around play activities.

ARCHITECT
The Design Forum Inc.

TYPE OF FACILITY
Early Childhood Learning Environment

TYPE OF CONSTRUCTION
New

SITE AREA
56 acres

BUILDING AREA
64,590 square feet

TOTAL PROJECT COST
$5,903,095

STATUS OF PROJECT
Completed January 1995

NUMBER OF STUDENTS
666

STRUCTURAL ENGINEER
Prein and Newhof

MECHANICAL/ELECTRICAL ENGINEER
The Design Forum Inc.

CONTRACTOR
Muskegon Construction

ELEMENTARY SCHOOLS

LONG BEACH INTERNATIONAL ELEMENTARY SCHOOL

HONOR   LONG BEACH, CALIFORNIA

ARCHITECT'S STATEMENT

Program: A large (1,100-student) elementary school in downtown Long Beach, California on a 2.5 acre site. The elementary schools in the area are extremely overcrowded due to an explosion of immigrant growth from Latin America and South-East Asia. With no land available, an arrangement was made between the school district and the Community Redevelopment Agency to build a school on this site.

Solution: The architects felt the program demanded a new prototype for urban schools. To maximize the site for educational facilities, the playfield was situated on an elevated concrete deck, 8 feet above street level. Lower grade classrooms, four kindergarten classrooms, a library, multipurpose room, and food service are located under the playdeck, 4 feet below street level. Administration is

located at the street-level entry overlooking a large open plaza at the lower classroom level. The plaza is large enough to assemble the entire school, serve as an informal amphitheater, and is dominated by a large photomural depicting the history of literature. Remaining classrooms are located in a three-story building that separates the playdeck and plaza from a heavily traveled downtown street.

Process: This building houses a program previously located in a temporary campus two blocks away. The existing educational program was well-established with strong community ties. The programming effort was led by the existing principal over a three-month period with school staff and some community input.

ARCHITECT
Thomas Blurock Architects, Inc.

ASSOCIATE ARCHITECT
Morphosis, Inc.

TYPE OF FACILITY
Elementary School

TYPE OF CONSTRUCTION
New

SITE AREA
2.5 acres

BUILDING AREA
79,605 square feet

TOTAL PROJECT COST
$17,299,838

STATUS OF PROJECT
Completed December 1998

NUMBER OF STUDENTS
1,100

STRUCTURAL/MECHANICAL/
ELECTRICAL ENGINEER
Ove Arup & Partners Inc.

CONTRACTOR
Multiple Prime Contract

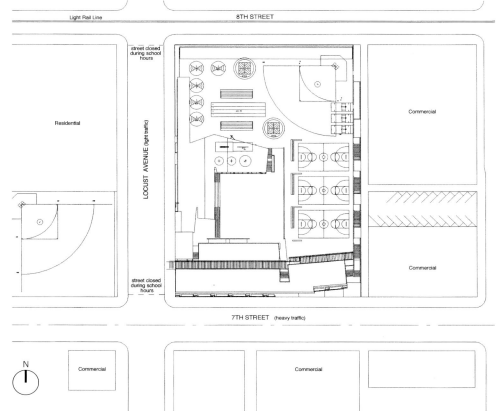

TENDERLOIN COMMUNITY SCHOOL

ARCHITECT'S STATEMENT

Through the efforts of a local community group, the public learned that over 1,000 elementary school children lived in this historically 'dangerous' neighborhood and were attending 47 different elementary schools throughout the city. In 1994, following a large-scale public awareness campaign, this project was funded through passage of Proposition A.

The architects drew design inspiration for the school from numerous focus group meetings with principals, teachers, parents, and children, as well as community members. It was the hope of the community that the school would become a new 'safe' symbol for the neighborhood. Challenging traditional notions of the school as closed fortress; the school, in its diverse program, strong community

influence, and physical design, 'opens' its doors to expose the innovation and learning happening within.

The building is an urban multi-use facility—an elementary school, pre-school, community center, and parking garage. Open rooftop playgrounds and a community garden were considered a priority since the children of the Tenderloin have little open play space in close proximity, and agriculture in many cases plays an important role in their cultures. The architectural design of video walls, graphics walls, areas for child-designed tiles, and display cases allows the children to exhibit and educate passers-by about the activities taking place inside the school.

ARCHITECT
**Esherick Homsey Dodge & Davis
(EHDD) in association with
Barcelon + Jang**

TYPE OF FACILITY
**Early Childhood Learning
Environment / Elementary School**

TYPE OF CONSTRUCTION
New

SITE AREA
31,630 acres

BUILDING AREA
85,488 square feet

TOTAL PROJECT COST
$20 M

STATUS OF PROJECT
Completed 1999

NUMBER OF STUDENTS
540+

STRUCTURAL ENGINEER
Structural Design Engineers

MECHANICAL ENGINEER
Tommy Siu Associates

ELECTRICAL ENGINEER
Pete O. Lapis & Associates

CONTRACTOR
Neilsen Dillingham Builders, Inc.

Elementary school
A   Rooftop community garden
B   Rooftop play yard
C   School bus stop
D   Driveway to parking
Adjacent uses
1   Restaurant
2   3-story office building

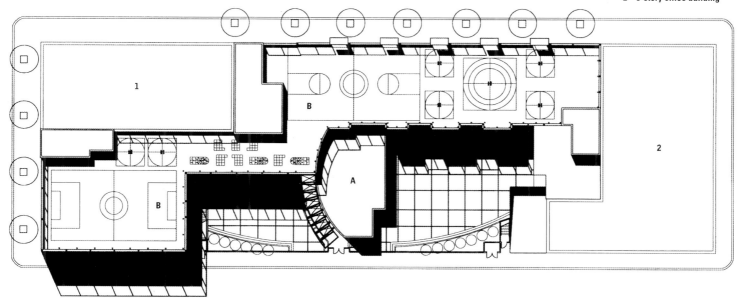

CESAR CHAVEZ ELEMENTARY SCHOOL

SAN DIEGO, CALIFORNIA

ARCHITECT'S STATEMENT

The eight-month community workshop effort had full participation from a broad variety of stakeholders. Beyond the stated mission for an elementary school, the 'genuine' needs of the community were far-reaching.

For decades this inner-city neighborhood has been without customary public services such as a community library, branch banks, clinics, grocery store, and so on. The new strategies: the multipurpose building 'expanded' to become an auditorium, cafeteria, lunch court, amphitheater, and music studio. The library 're-invented' itself to include a small theater and a leisure reading lounge with a fireplace.

The pictographic images throughout the campus are derived from 25,000 years of oral storytelling traditions of the Americas. In using a storytelling approach for the generation of form, the new school immediately captures the emotional and cultural heritage of its student body, which is 98 percent Hispanic. This can be seen in the academic plaza, where a 350 foot long Cosmic Indian is dressed in the cultural milestones of the Americas. The main façade of the library depicts the logo of the United Farm Workers in ruby red granite. Taken together, the library-administration building forms Kukulcan, the most powerful deity in the Mayan universe.

ARCHITECT
Martinez + Cutri

TYPE OF FACILITY
Elementary School

TYPE OF CONSTRUCTION
New

SITE AREA
7.9 acres

BUILDING AREA
46,100 square feet

TOTAL PROJECT COST
$9,880,600

STATUS OF PROJECT
Completed March 1998

NUMBER OF STUDENTS
600

STRUCTURAL ENGINEER
Flores Consulting Group

MECHANICAL ENGINEER
Sevier-Siskovic Engineers

ELECTRICAL ENGINEER
KANRAD Engineering

CONTRACTOR
DEB Inc.

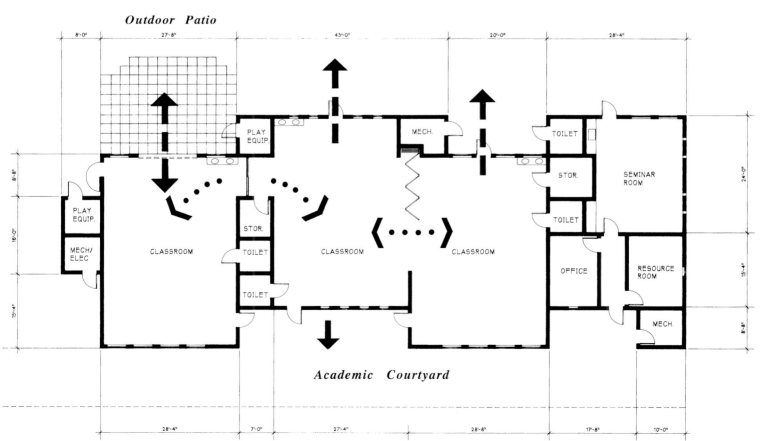

Outdoor Patio

Academic Courtyard

UNIVERSITY ELEMENTARY SCHOOL

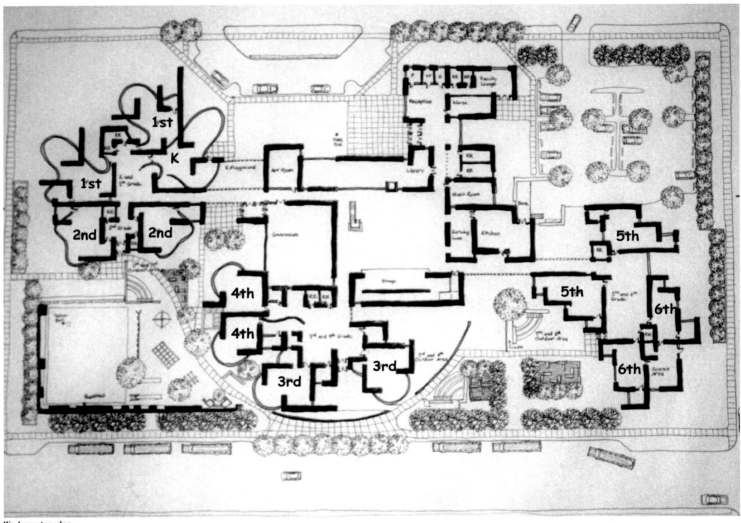

Kindergarten plan

DESIGNER'S STATEMENT

The true challenge of designing schools lies in creating a space that will not become obsolete after a few years and a few different teaching techniques. Designing schools for the unchanging characteristics of children enables them to last longer.

A lot is known about how the physical environment affects children—emotionally, psychologically, and intellectually. This knowledge should be used to form their learning spaces. Children develop at different paces, but most develop at the same rate within a two-year span of each other.

Since children have different learning patterns at varying ages, they have different ideal learning environments at each of these ages. No two grade levels should have classrooms which are exactly alike. At the same time, children need a sense of

continuity and security. Each learning environment they progress through should have similarities to tie their experiences together.

Architects must be willing to see the world through the eyes of a child if we are to have productive and lasting learning environments for our children.

Most important concepts:

Kindergarten

- Multiple areas to help with attention span, and identifiable spaces
- Need whole class, small group, and individual areas
- Use repetitive, predictable patterning
- Use organized entry sequence

Third grade

- Reveal 'meaning' of environment

- Use a variety and quantity of display areas
- Parent conference areas very important
- Use unique, identifiable, and yet unclaimable spaces
- Each child should have his/her own storage area

Sixth grade

- Do not use 'instigating' colors
- Need places to display final, not process, products
- Need peer mediation space
- Flexible space with delicate detailing
- Need 'claimable' and 'unclaimable' spaces

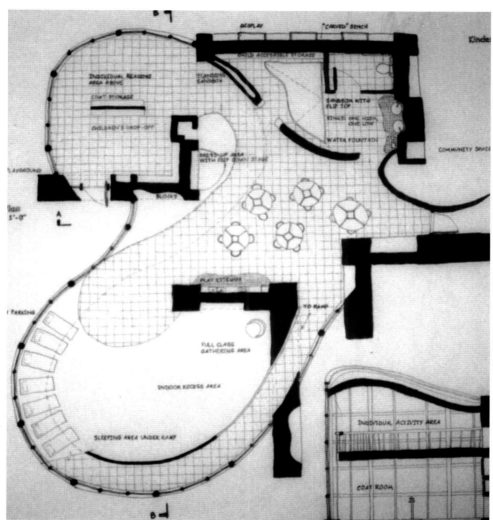

Sixth grade plan

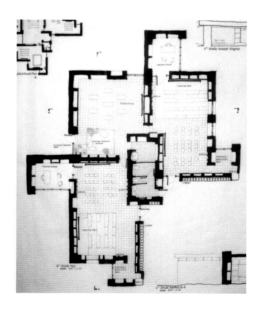

DESIGNER
Bridgett R. Wakefield, University of Illinois, Urbana Champaign

TYPE OF FACILITY
Elementary School / Unique Learning Environment

TYPE OF CONSTRUCTION
New / Thesis

NUMBER OF STUDENTS
344

SITE AREA
4.9 acres

BUILDING AREA
34,400 square feet

TOTAL PROJECT COST
Est. $8 M

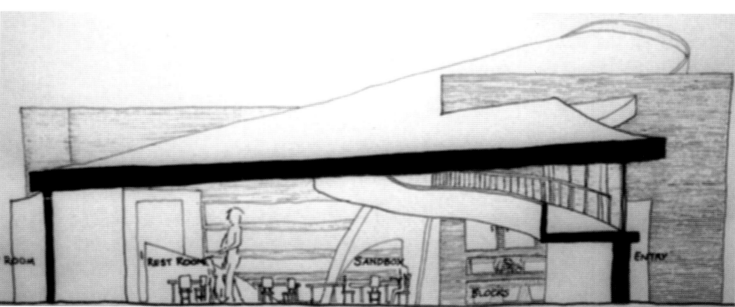

Kindergarten section

WILBERT SNOW ELEMENTARY SCHOOL

MIDDLETOWN, CONNECTICUT

ARCHITECT'S STATEMENT

Located on a thickly wooded site, the school has been designed to integrate indoor and outdoor learning environments. The original school was a seven-building campus that allowed children close contact with the beautiful site, but resulted in lost instructional time in bad weather. A single structure now connects the existing gymnasium, auditorium, and a reprogrammed classroom building while maintaining the experience of walking through the woods on the way to class. The remains of an 18th-century road believed to be the location of a town meeting with George Washington passes through the site. At different points it becomes an outdoor learning center, playground, and the main lobby of the school. A pedestrian bridge from the main building allows protected passage to the new dining hall while maintaining neighborhood access to the recreational amenities of the site. Instructional areas are each identified by signage and cast-stone medallions representing plants and animals found on the site. Wood, masonry, and glass form a palette of materials that further connects the built environment to the natural one.

ARCHITECT
Jeter, Cook & Jepson Architects, Inc.

TYPE OF FACILITY
Early Childhood Learning Environment / Elementary School

TYPE OF CONSTRUCTION
Addition/Renovation

SITE AREA
14.5 acres

BUILDING AREA
71,600 square feet

TOTAL PROJECT COST
$9.8 M

STATUS OF PROJECT
Completed 1998

NUMBER OF STUDENTS
550

STRUCTURAL ENGINEER
Girard & Company, Engineers

MECHANICAL/ELECTRICAL ENGINEER
Bemis Associates

CONTRACTOR
Haynes Construction Company

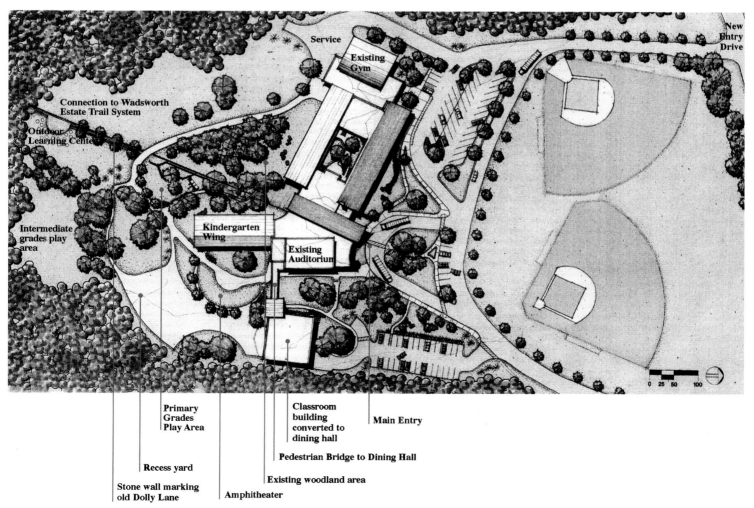

Connection to Wadsworth Estate Trail System

Outdoor Learning Center

New Entry Drive

Service

Existing Gym

Intermediate grades play area

Kindergarten Wing

Existing Auditorium

Primary Grades Play Area

Classroom building converted to dining hall

Main Entry

Recess yard

Pedestrian Bridge to Dining Hall

Stone wall marking old Dolly Lane

Existing woodland area

Amphitheater

0 25 50 100

BENJAMIN FRANKLIN ELEMENTARY SCHOOL

MERIDEN, CONNECTICUT

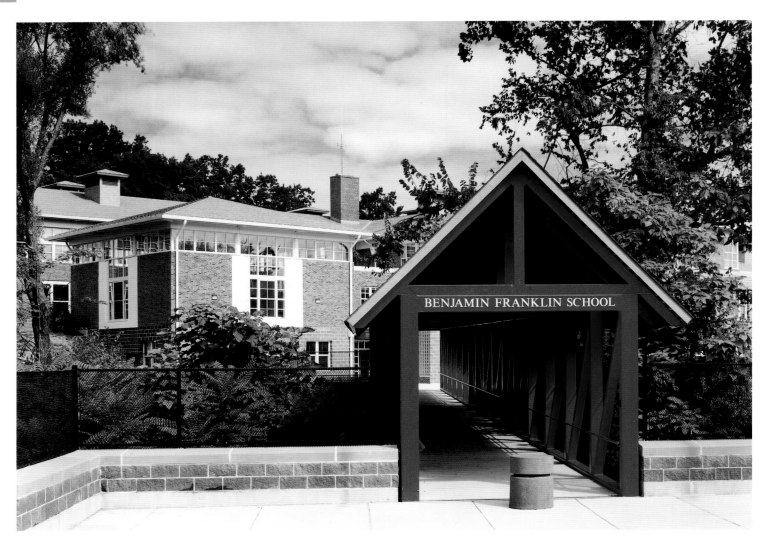

ARCHITECT'S STATEMENT

The Benjamin Franklin School included a major renovation and addition to a 1950's era building located in an urban setting. The major components included a complete interior renovation, replacement of all the windows to change the scale and character of the building to be more in keeping with the large homes in the existing neighborhood, and the addition of a pitched roof. A pedestrian bridge crosses a brook and surrounding wetlands area to reach town-owned land, which became additional parking, a drop-off area and a

grassy play area. These features were not present due to the tight urban nature of the site. The bridge not only provides access to the other side, it also allows students a glimpse into an active wetlands habitat. The bridge was painted a bright red, which is reminiscent of a nearby landmark called the Old Red Bridge. In addition to renovating the existing school, a three-story addition was built, which contains a new cafeteria, media center, art and music rooms, and classrooms.

ARCHITECT
**Jeter, Cook & Jepson
Architects, Inc.**

TYPE OF FACILITY
Elementary School

TYPE OF CONSTRUCTION
Addition / Renovation

SITE AREA
5.9 acres

BUILDING AREA
74,300 square feet

TOTAL PROJECT COST
$13.3 M

STATUS OF PROJECT
Completed 1998

NUMBER OF STUDENTS
600

STRUCTURAL ENGINEER
Girard & Company Engineers

MECHANICAL/ELECTRICAL
ENGINEER
Legnos & Cramer, Inc.

CONTRACTOR
P. Francini & Company

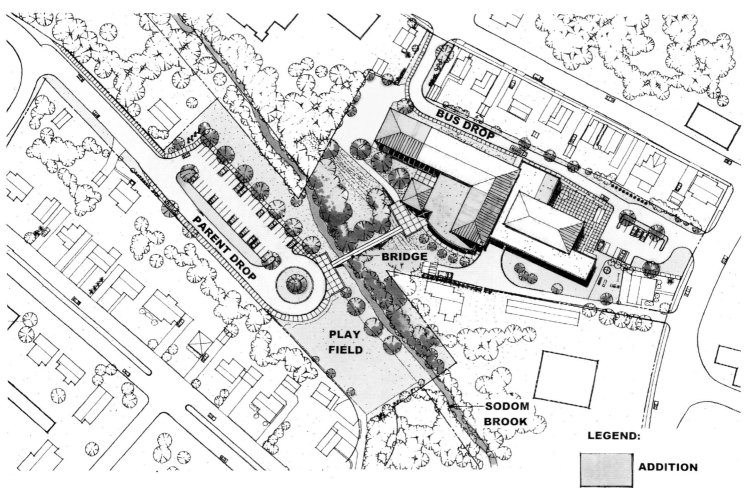

BUS DROP

PARENT DROP

BRIDGE

PLAY
FIELD

SODOM
BROOK

LEGEND:

ADDITION

CLAIRE LILIENTHAL ELEMENTARY SCHOOL

SAN FRANCISCO, CALIFORNIA

ARCHITECT'S STATEMENT

Claire Lilienthal School is a very successful K–8 alternative public school in San Francisco, founded by teachers and families who wanted an opportunity to collaborate in all facets of their children's education. Families, staff, and neighbors have developed a unique sense of belonging to a close community who all feel responsibility for the children's growth and wellbeing. Our goal in building a new facility for the K–2 program was to express and reinforce the sense of nurturing that characterizes the school. The Madison Campus houses 240 students on a 1 acre site. Our project replaced bungalows placed on the site 'temporarily' in the 1970s with permanent buildings housing classrooms, a library, and the school administration. A lovely existing auditorium and two-classroom kindergarten wing were maintained. The new buildings complete a courtyard that the existing L-shaped building began.

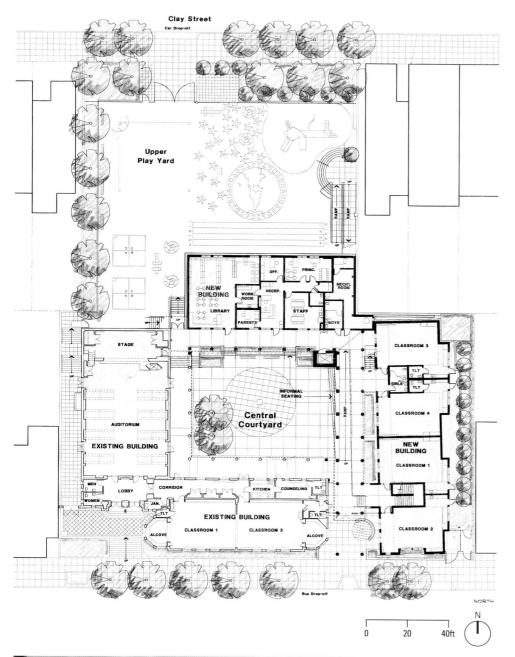

Clay Street
Car Drop-off

Upper
Play Yard

NEW BUILDING

OFF.

PRINC.

WORK ROOM

RECEP.

MECH'L ROOM

LIBRARY

STAFF

PARENTS'

BOYS'

UP

RAMP   RAMP

UP

STAGE

UP

AUDITORIUM

EXISTING BUILDING

Central Courtyard

INFORMAL SEATING

RAMP

UP

CLASSROOM 3

TLT

GIRLS'

TLT

CLASSROOM 4

NEW BUILDING

CLASSROOM 1

MEN

WOMEN

LOBBY

CORRIDOR

JAN.

TLT

KITCHEN

COUNSELING

TLT

ALCOVE

EXISTING BUILDING

CLASSROOM 1   CLASSROOM 2

ALCOVE

TLT

CLASSROOM 2

UP

Bus Drop-off

NORTH

0   20   40ft

N

ARCHITECT
Gelfand RNP Architects

TYPE OF FACILITY
Elementary School / Alternative School

TYPE OF CONSTRUCTION
Addition / Renovation

SITE AREA
1 acre

BUILDING AREA
24,264 square feet

TOTAL PROJECT COST
$3,850,000

STATUS OF PROJECT
Completed 1998

NUMBER OF STUDENTS
240

STRUCTURAL ENGINEER
Biggs Cardosa Associates

MECHANICAL ENGINEER
MHC Engineers

ELECTRICAL ENGINEER
SCE Engineers

CONTRACTOR
Angotti & Reilly Construction

Haggerty School

Architect's statement

On a tight site, the challenge was to double the size and capacity of the school while preserving the character of the existing building and the scale of the residential area. Primary needs included the creation of new core facilities, integration of latest information technology, and securing of the school during community activities after hours.

After studying possible renovations and additions, it was determined that a new building would be most advantageous and cost-effective. In an inclusive six-month process, meetings were held to hear the concerns of residents opposed to demolition. As a result, the exterior of the new building echoes that of the old. The interior, however, is tailored to fulfil the needs of a 21st-century learning environment, with a fully integrated library/media center at its heart.

The design features a corridor encircling the gym that doubles as an acoustic barrier and viewing balcony. Roof monitors reflect glare-free daylight into the gym while enclosing a rooftop playground.

The result is a compact modern building that is easy to navigate and offers a calm, nurturing, non-institutional environment that is unusual in a public school.

1 Main front entry terrace for pick-up and drop-off
2 Side entrances for community access after hours
3 Open rooftop play area enclosed by light monitors
4 Play area
5 Parking area

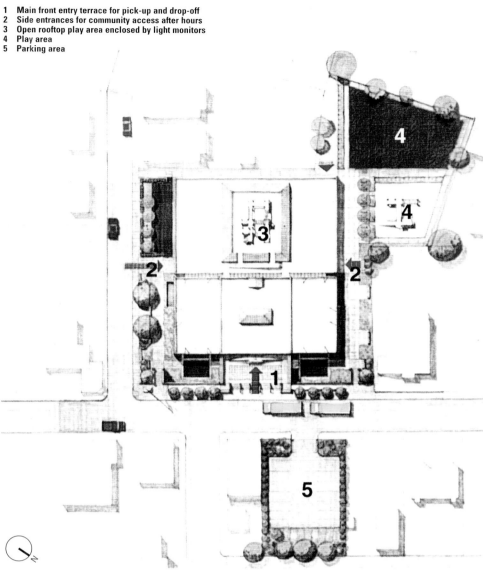

ARCHITECT
The Office of Michael Rosenfeld, Inc.

TYPE OF FACILITY
Elementary School

TYPE OF CONSTRUCTION
New

NUMBER OF STUDENTS
350

SITE AREA
1 acre

BUILDING AREA
54,500 square feet

TOTAL PROJECT COST
$9.5 M

STATUS OF PROJECT
Completed 1995

STRUCTURAL ENGINEER
Engineers Design Group Inc.

MECHANICAL/ELECTRICAL ENGINEER
Shooshanian Engineering Associates, Inc.

CONTRACTOR
J. P. Construction Inc.

JAMES F. OYSTER ELEMENTARY SCHOOL

ARCHITECT'S STATEMENT

A new 45,000 square foot school facility replaces the original 1926 James F. Oyster Elementary School with a new Oyster Bilingual School. The Oyster Bilingual School is a multicultural school where all instruction takes place in both Spanish and English. The instructional program drove the design of the school. Because instruction in every class takes place in two languages, the classroom required two distinct teaching walls that could be viewed from the same student area. This drove the 'L-shaped' classrooms with dual 'primary' teaching walls. The design solution, as well as other solutions, was validated and tested through school/community consensus meetings throughout the design process.

The architectural design is intended to reflect the rich diversity of this Washington neighborhood's heritage. A Federalist façade with columned portico and copula dominated the exterior design, while Spanish tiles and color schemes graced the interior, reflecting the bilingual focus. The original school included 10 classrooms, occupying 28,000 square feet.

Funding was provided by a creative partnership with the private sector apartment development. This necessitated an urban arrangement of multi-level classrooms, including an underground parking structure buffered from the new living development. The scope of work included demolition of the original structures, and construction of a new educational facility to provide 21 classrooms including art, music, and a community service area housing the

school's cafeteria and media center for after-hours use by the neighboring community.

This project, managed by the public and private partnership, delivered the first new school for the District of Columbia in 20 years.

ARCHITECT
Jacobs Facilities Inc.

TYPE OF FACILITY
Elementary School

TYPE OF CONSTRUCTION
New

SITE AREA
.82 acres

BUILDING AREA
45,000 square feet

TOTAL PROJECT COST
$10.1 M

STATUS OF PROJECT
Completed July 2001

NUMBER OF STUDENTS
350

STRUCTURAL/MECHANICAL/
ELECTRICAL ENGINEER
Jacobs Facilities Inc.

CONTRACTOR
Donohoe Construction

NON-PROFIT PARTNER
**The 21st Century School Fund
with funding from the Ford
Foundation**

DEVELOPER
LCOR, Inc

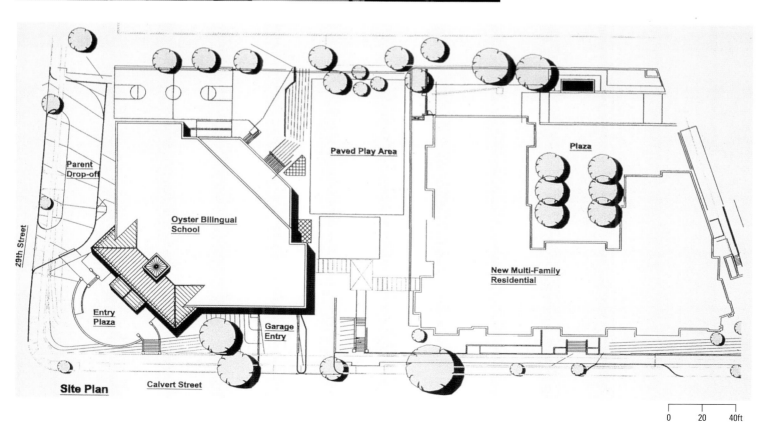

Site Plan

Parent Drop-off

Oyster Bilingual School

Entry Plaza

Garage Entry

Paved Play Area

Plaza

New Multi-Family Residential

29th Street

Calvert Street

0   20   40ft

LONGMEADOW CENTER ELEMENTARY SCHOOL

LONGMEADOW, MASSACHUSETTS

ARCHITECT'S STATEMENT

Situated on the historic Town Green, the existing K–4 elementary school consisted of two buildings separated by a residential street. The children crossed the road for lunch, library, and gym class. The local Historic District Commission required that any addition could not be visible from the Green and that existing façades, visible from a public road, could not be altered.

Our publicly endorsed design solution re-routed the road around the site and manipulated the topography to facilitate a below-grade addition connecting the buildings. The addition, consisting of a new media center, technology laboratory, teacher facilities, and connecting corridor, is not visible from the historic Green. Creative landscaping masks the masonry plaza above the addition as it is used for group gatherings and a safe exterior connection between the two buildings.

A second floor, inserted into the upper level of the original two-story space of the circa 1920 building, houses new fourth grade classrooms. Additionally, new spaces were created for pre-kindergarten classes (including a common area), art, music, special needs, a cafeteria, and a kitchen. All building systems were replaced, a LAN was installed through the facility, and the playground area more than doubled in size.

This design solution not only fulfils the town's, state's and Historic District Commission's requirements, it also brings together the past, present, and future in a facility that preserves history as well as displays the town's commitment to quality education.

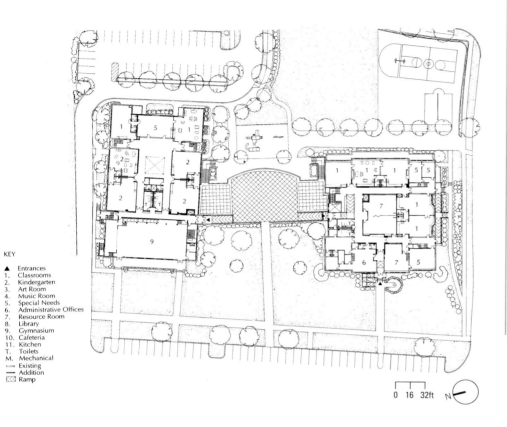

KEY
▲ Entrances
1. Classrooms
2. Kindergarten
3. Art Room
4. Music Room
5. Special Needs
6. Administrative Offices
7. Resource Room
8. Library
9. Gymnasium
10. Cafeteria
11. Kitchen
T. Toilets
M. Mechanical
⚊ Existing
— Addition
▧ Ramp

0   16   32ft   N

ARCHITECT
Tappé Associates, Inc.

TYPE OF FACILITY
Elementary School

TYPE OF CONSTRUCTION
Addition/Renovation

NUMBER OF STUDENTS
625

SITE AREA
4.6 acres

BUILDING AREA
81,500 square feet

TOTAL PROJECT COST
$11.5 M

STATUS OF PROJECT
Completed 1997

STRUCTURAL ENGINEER
Veitas & Veitas, Inc.

MECHANICAL ENGINEER
Electrical Energy Auditor & Consultants

ELECTRICAL ENGINEER
Robert Hall Consulting Engineers

CONTRACTOR
Fontaine Brothers, Inc.

MEREDITH HILL ELEMENTARY SCHOOL

AUBURN, WASHINGTON

ARCHITECT'S STATEMENT

The school is nestled on a square 10 acre hillside parcel within a suburban neighborhood overlooking Rainier Valley cities, with the Cascade Mountain range behind. The 53,500 square foot, two-story building was set into the southeast slope to improve residential views and free up land for outdoor activities. Light-colored façades, terraced levels, pathway networks, and landscape buffers enhance the community fit.

With a $103/square foot building budget, value engineering and constructability review processes aided in meeting advanced site improvements and technology systems at a winning bid of only $97/square foot. The unique lobby, wedged between two tall building systems, provides an inexpensive large-volume commons space that eliminates narrow connecting halls and stairs. By careful use of the code to full advantage, the sprinklered building with mixed occupancies, incorporates the concept of classroom and commons at both levels on grade, resulting in a school with few fire rated corridors, and few door closers, most rooms with direct access to outside, and no area separation walls.

The compact plan satisfies the educational program for easily accessible (ADA) educational space for multi-aged groupings and cross-aged tutoring on both levels. Classrooms are equitable in size, but provide flexibility to facilitate several different teaching styles for now and the future. Support offices are located on each level within the lobby, so students, parents, and staff can easily reach counselors, therapist, psychologists, language specialist, and other instructional assistants.

In the heart of the school is the award-winning lobby, which has physical and visual circulation and connection to the classroom levels and the assembly spaces. Riser seating, low display cases, and multimedia technology encourage its multi-use as an education, relaxation, and assembly space, for which waiting lists develop. Adjoining spaces can open individually or in combination with other rooms so many special-use arrangements can be accomplished while maintaining security to the rest of the school.

ARCHITECT
Gregory & Chapel Architects PS

TYPE OF FACILITY
Early Childhood Learning Environment / Elementary School / Innovative Learning Environment / Other or Multipurpose

TYPE OF CONSTRUCTION
New

SITE AREA
10 acres

BUILDING AREA
53,531 square feet

TOTAL PROJECT COST
$6.5 M

STATUS OF PROJECT
Completed August 1995

NUMBER OF STUDENTS
550

STRUCTURAL ENGINEER
Peterson Strehle, Martinson, Inc.

MECHANICAL/ELECTRICAL ENGINEER
HEI Hargis Engineers Inc.

CONTRACTOR
Berschauer Phillips Construction Co. Inc.

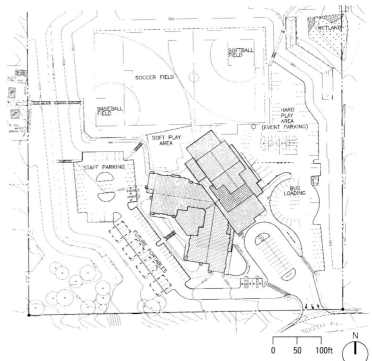

MORGAN HILL COUNTRY SCHOOL

Morgan Hill Country School
Site Diagram

1 Soccer Field
2 Pool
3 Orchard
4 Caretaker's Residence
5 Multipurpose Room/Gym
6 Outdoor Stage
7 Playground
8 Science Classrooms
9 Art & Music Classrooms
10 Academic Quad
11 Typical Outdoor Classroom
12 Middle School (Grades 6-8)
13 Elementary School (Grades 1-5)
14 Early Childhood (Grades 4yrs-K)
15 Early Childhood Playyard
16 Library
17 Computer Lab
18 Extended Care
19 Olive Tree Alee
20 Administration
21 Founder's Walk
22 Oak Grove Parking

ARCHITECT'S STATEMENT

Morgan Hill Country School is a 425-student, pre-K through eighth grade private school located on a 10 acre site in the agricultural outskirts of Morgan Hill, California. This school is operated by A Gifted Education, Inc., a non-profit educational corporation which also operates the Almaden Country School in San Jose, California.

Site selection began in 1996, final site selection occurred in December 1999, and design and construction were phased over the next two years. The complete campus opened in the fall of 1999.

The greatest challenge for this school was to design a facility that supported the vision put forth by the strong leadership of the director, Steve Hayden. He wanted a school with a 'country' atmosphere that supported the school's philosophy of 'a gifted education for every child.'

Since this was the first ground-up campus to be developed by the non-profit corporation, we engaged in three levels of programming. First, the core educational program was developed with the director and principal (prior to site selection). Second, after the site was selected, we sponsored a hands-on design charrette with teachers and administrators to address specific site issues, adjacencies, and to develop site plan alternatives. And third, we sponsored a series of workshops with parents, teachers, and community members to address concerns and present the evolving design.

These three programming levels allowed us to engage the client and community in the complexities of the process (which included widening a local highway, installing a new traffic signal, and making a new street), and provided us with key

insights about the school that we might not otherwise have discovered. Although we have designed many schools, the process gave us a unique understanding of this particular organization as a community.

The resulting design is a unique mix of building types: large barn-like structures for the administration, library and gymnasium/theatre, low-slung energy-efficient classrooms, and a 'farm-house' for the extended care facility. The buildings are extensively integrated in the landscape, including native vegetation and drought-tolerant landscaping, outdoor classrooms, a kitchen/agricultural garden (developed in conjunction with master gardeners of the region), and an indoor/outdoor stage.

ARCHITECT
Bridges Architecture

TYPE OF FACILITY
Early Childhood Learning Environment / Elementary School / Middle/Junior High School / Innovative Learning Environment / Other or Multipurpose / Master Plan

TYPE OF CONSTRUCTION
New

SITE AREA
12 acres

BUILDING AREA
50,000 square feet

TOTAL PROJECT COST
$12 M

STATUS OF PROJECT
Phase I, June 1999

NUMBER OF STUDENTS
425

STRUCTURAL ENGINEER
Structural Design Engineers

MECHANICAL ENGINEER
Superior Heating and Sheet Metal

ELECTRICAL ENGINEER
Hayward Electric

CONTRACTOR
Lyons constructions

MOYLAN ELEMENTARY SCHOOL

ARCHITECT'S STATEMENT

The city required renovation and major expansion of a neglected 1920's school on a 3.15 acre site to accommodate 600 K–6 students in a safe and welcoming environment. Several months of programming discussions resulted in the design of an L-shaped addition totaling 98,000 square feet and renovation of the existing 50,000 square feet. The addition created a central courtyard, underground parking, and a new main entrance on a side street.

Perceived as the focal point in the design, the enclosed courtyard ensures a safe and fun environment for outdoor recreational and educational activities before, during, and after school. The L-shaped addition includes a new library, auditorium, cafeteria, and new classrooms, all of which look out onto the courtyard. Classrooms

and corridors that face the courtyard have high glass-to-wall ratio, creating a transparent quality between courtyard and school interiors.

The existing building was renovated to reflect the original era of construction, retaining its high ceilings and large, double-hung windows, while making it 100 percent handicapped accessible and fully wired for computers and multimedia instruction.

Special attention was given to making core facilities such as the library and the auditorium accessible and suitable for district-wide and local community use. The first in a city-wide school re-building program, the objective was to create a state-of-the-art, community-oriented neighborhood school with a warm and welcoming atmosphere.

ARCHITECT
Tai Soo Kim Partners

TYPE OF FACILITY
Elementary School

TYPE OF CONSTRUCTION
Addition/Renovation

NUMBER OF STUDENTS
600

SITE AREA
3.15 acres

TOTAL PROJECT COST
$21.9 M

STATUS OF PROJECT
Completed 1994

STRUCTURAL ENGINEER
Santo Domingo Engineering

MECHANICAL/ELECTRICAL
ENGINEER
Quinlan, Giannoni & Livingston, Inc.

CONTRACTOR
Newfield Construction

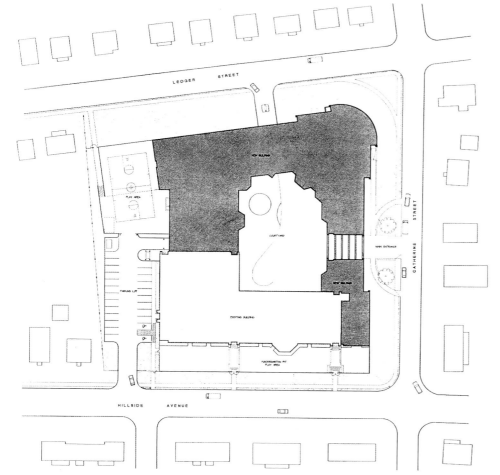

NELDA MUNDY ELEMENTARY SCHOOL

FAIRFIELD, CALIFORNIA

ARCHITECT'S STATEMENT

The program called for a prototypical year-round school serving grades K–6 with a daily population of 650 students. Goals included: unobtrusive building security; a supportive learning environment; state-of-the-art technology; and a strong and child-friendly identity.

Architects and educators met in a series of workshops over three months to develop the design. Alternative designs were discussed with the community, with the school board, and with design team members throughout the design process. A design was selected and completed within another six months. Team members met regularly to assure that they adhered to project goals.

The finished design achieved these goals. Buildings form a secure triangular courtyard with attractive metal gates between buildings. Classroom design and lighting support the educational mission. A data and communications system connects the school to the rest of the world. Steep roofs and curved and sinuous entrance canopies create a strong identity for the school. Bright colors and playful curving forms give students the knowledge that it is their school.

ARCHITECT
VBN Architects

TYPE OF FACILITY
Elementary School

TYPE OF CONSTRUCTION
New

SITE AREA
7 acres

BUILDING AREA
48,076 square feet

TOTAL PROJECT COST
$8,073,000

STATUS OF PROJECT
Completed July 1998

NUMBER OF STUDENTS
750

STRUCTURAL ENGINEER
Dominic Chu

MECHANICAL/ELECTRICAL
ENGINEER
**Murakami, Myer & Horn Assoc.,
Inc.**

CONTRACTOR
West Coast Contractor Inc.

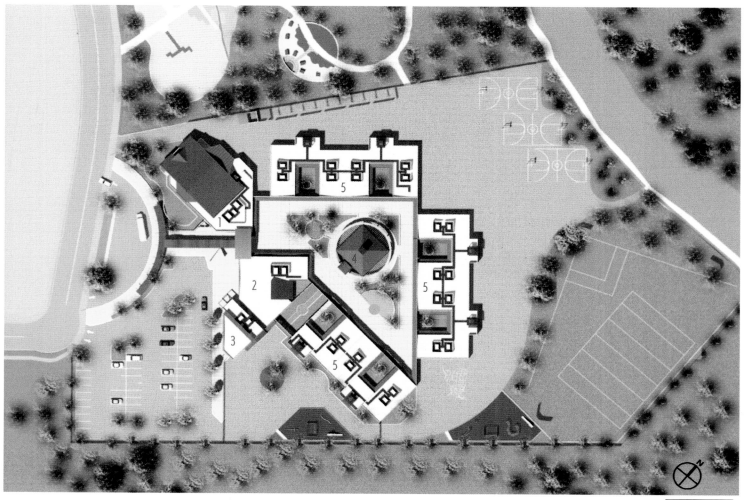

0   40   80ft

NORTH STAR ELEMENTARY

ARCHITECT'S STATEMENT

The program for the first new elementary school to be built in this school district in 18 years, while based at the beginning of the project on older District models, was transformed through the design process into a current, progressive, technologically responsive model for the new millennium. The process involved weekly meetings with the multiple District personnel, educators, and public representatives. Tours of other projects and several meetings with the general community over a three-month period, provided great insight and design resources for the architects.

Priorities identified as critical to the project included the need to break down the large scale of the 30-classroom, 72,000 square foot program, and the desire for a building that would facilitate flexibility in

curriculum, use of technology, and a wide variety of teaching strategies. Also high priorities were the ability to utilize the building and the site as learning tools, the presentation of the physical building as exciting, playful, and appealing for children, and the use of lasting and durable materials and building systems.

The entire school is designed to encourage learning in all aspects of a student's life—not just the classroom—to encourage life-long learning.

ARCHITECT
Valentiner Crane Brunjes Onyon Architects

TYPE OF FACILITY
Elementary School / Innovative Learning Environment

TYPE OF CONSTRUCTION
New

SITE AREA
12 acres

BUILDING AREA
72,308 square feet

TOTAL PROJECT COST
$7,810,371

STATUS OF PROJECT
Completed 1999

STRUCTURAL ENGINEER
Bsumek-Mu & Associates

MECHANICAL ENGINEER
Olsen & Peterson Engineers

ELECTRICAL ENGINEER
BNA Consulting Engineers II

CONTRACTOR
Herm Hughs and Sons

floor plan

1. ENTRY
2. ADMINISTRATION
3. GYM/MULTI PURPOSE
3a. STAGE
4. CAFETERIA
5. KITCHEN
6. STORAGE/MECHANICAL
7. N SCHOOL ALTERNATIVE
8. MEDIA CENTER
9. MEDIA SUPPORT
10. ESL/ALP
11. OUTDOOR CLASS ROOM
12. MUSIC
13. TEACHER PREP AREA
14. REST ROOMS (STUDENT)
15. COAT RM

P.S. 56/The Louis DeSario Elementary School

STATEN ISLAND, NEW YORK

ARCHITECT'S STATEMENT

As the first new school to be built in this severely overcrowded district in nearly two decades, the local school district and surrounding community were key constituents in the programming/planning process. Overcrowding in the schools was such a serious concern that a district-wide moratorium on new housing construction was imposed within the community until the new school could be built.

The primary needs were for a 900-seat K–5 school that could also be used after hours for a wide range of community events. The initial program called for six kindergarten classrooms, 15 first, second, and third grade classrooms, 10 fourth and fifth grade classrooms, and three special education classrooms, together with a 450-seat multipurpose auditorium, gymnasium, and cafeteria.

From the earliest stages, the architect and local school district representatives visited buildings which were considered prototypes by team members. With these structures in mind, a continuing dialogue was established to allow for these ideas to be adapted to meet the specifics of this program. Modifications included increasing the area of the gymnasium and cafeteria, placement of the gym and playground to take advantage of the site, and ideas from early childhood experts regarding the design elements of the outdoor playground. As a result of this up-front inclusion of all constituents, the initial design submission was warmly received by the community and passed on its first review.

ARCHITECT
Mitchell/Giurgola Architects, LLP

TYPE OF FACILITY
Elementary School

TYPE OF CONSTRUCTION
New

SITE AREA
2.9 acres

BUILDING AREA
99,018 square feet

TOTAL PROJECT COST
$35,225,000

STATUS OF PROJECT
Completed May 1998

NUMBER OF STUDENTS
900

STRUCTURAL ENGINEER
Ysrael A. Seinuk, P.C.

MECHANICAL/ELECTRICAL
ENGINEER
DVL Consulting Engineers, Inc.

CONTRACTOR
Turner Construction Company

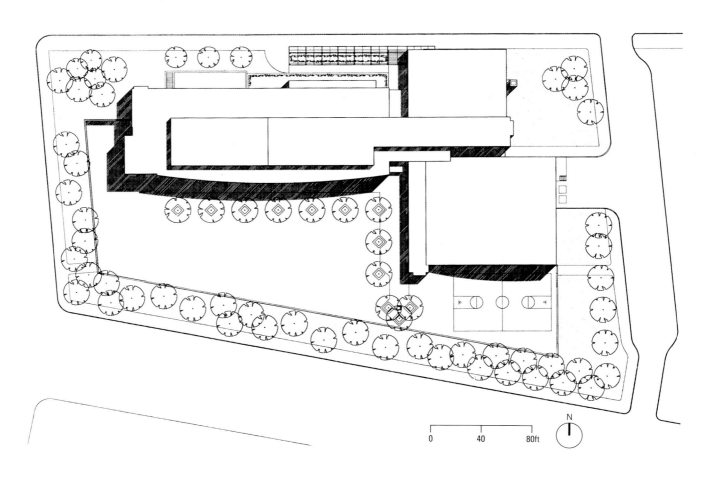

0   40   80ft

N

ELEMENTARY SCHOOLS

SALTONSTALL ELEMENTARY SCHOOL

ARCHITECT'S STATEMENT

Built in 1915, and sited one block from the New England coast, this 64,000 square foot middle school was converted to a pre-K through fifth grade elementary school for 520 students. A 20,000 square foot addition and an extensive renovation of the existing building supports a year-round innovative curriculum where students attend classes in six-week sessions with two-week breaks in between. The school operates on the educational philosophy of 'multiple intelligences' (MI) requiring the design of numerous spaces for multipurpose activities that focus on different aspects of students' intellectual growth.

The program includes 21 classrooms, two pre-K rooms, a cafeteria, a health area, faculty dining room and kitchen, a media center, parent center, science discovery center, a large music room, 25-seat computer lab, art room, gymnasium, and an auditorium.

Renovations to the existing facility included entirely new mechanical, electrical, and plumbing systems; a new roof; and a complete refurbishment of interior spaces, including new casework and sinks in each classroom; new finishes; and complete upgrades to meet all current building, life safety, and accessibility codes.

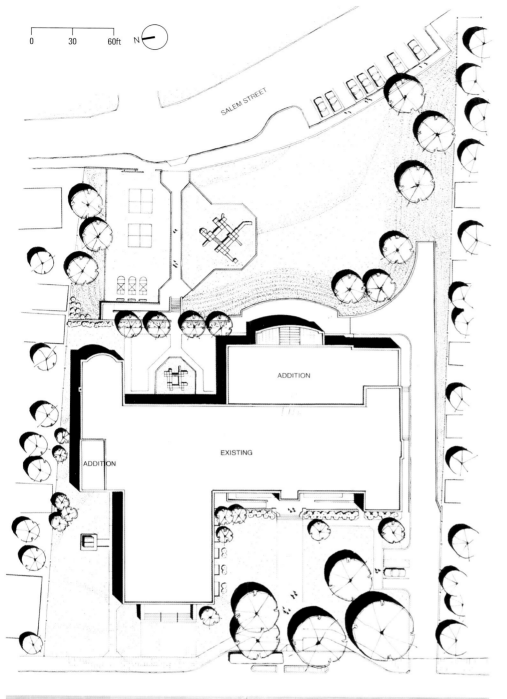

ARCHITECT
Flansburgh Associates, Inc.

TYPE OF FACILITY
Early Childhood Learning Environment / Elementary School / Alternative School

TYPE OF CONSTRUCTION
Addition/Renovation

SITE AREA
2.4 acres

BUILDING AREA
84,000 square feet

TOTAL PROJECT COST
$8,077,654

STATUS OF PROJECT
Completed March 1996

NUMBER OF STUDENTS
520

STRUCTURAL ENGINEER
Engineers Design Group, Inc.

MECHANICAL ENGINEER
TMP Consulting Engineers

ELECTRICAL ENGINEER
Lottero & Mason Associates, Inc.

CONTRACTOR
TLT Construction Corporation

WHITTIER COMMUNITY SCHOOL FOR THE ARTS

ARCHITECT'S STATEMENT

The Whittier Community School for the Arts is located in the center of a neighborhood on the edge of downtown. The building is organized to maximize open space and fit within the adjacent residential context. Programmatically, the school serves as an educational center and as a neighborhood community facility. A partnership was formed with a neighboring art school and existing community resources.

Materials include brick, metal roofing, and stone detail that architecturally reflect the character and detail found in the neighborhood and vertical elements found in adjacent structures. These elements are incorporated within the school as stairs, ventilation shafts, and chases. This creates a structural sense of place, time, and permanence in the major public center.

Below the two floors of classrooms there is centralized parking. The mechanical systems are located in a specially designed attic. The building systems are located above the areas of usage with vertical connections for efficiency. State-of-the-art technology, indoor air quality, and system controls are monitored from a central computerized control at the off-site district headquarters.

The organization of interior spaces is along a linear path with a central entry and gathering space. The central space serves as an activity, gathering, and reception area for the school. The school's academic focus is reflected in the performance activities, art exhibitions, and instrumental music by volunteers that occur in this space.

Whittier School provides an urban identity for the neighborhood. The exterior spaces and interior gathering areas have made the building a primary public center for the entire community.

ARCHITECT
Kodet Architectural Group, Ltd.

TYPE OF FACILITY
Elementary (K–5)

TYPE OF CONSTRUCTION
New

SITE AREA
6.083 acres

BUILDING AREA
82,350 square feet

TOTAL PROJECT COST
$17,286,290

STATUS OF PROJECT
Completed January 1998

NUMBER OF STUDENTS
540/625

CIVIL/STRUCTURAL ENGINEER
Clark Engineering Corporation

MECHANICAL/ELECTRICAL ENGINEER
Michaud Cooley Erickson

CONTRACTOR
Shaw-Lundquist

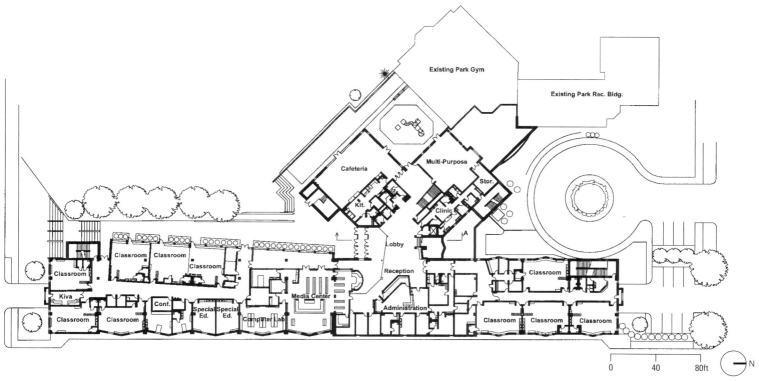

ELEMENTARY SCHOOLS

WHITTIER ELEMENTARY SCHOOL

SEATTLE, WASHINGTON

ARCHITECT'S STATEMENT

Tasked by the School Board with building a 'neighborhood school,' DLR Group met with 15 school and community members for a brainstorming session to kick off the collaborative design process. At a design workshop the committee establishes design goals by identifying aspects they like from three dramatically different design concepts developed by DLR Group. A desire to organize the school around a strong central space with a fun architectural image best conveyed the school's educational philosophy of innovative learning within a structured environment.

Excitement for the new school grew when imagery from the local ship canal was incorporated into architectural elements creating a custom fit between the school and its neighborhood. The 'canal' concept created opportunities for the design team to meet district building standards and

educational goals in creative ways. The library reading room became a gatehouse, schools of metal fish provide safety at the bridge, and a kelp forest of metal and cork serves as a backdrop for student artwork.

The collaborative design process creates a symbiosis. The school has taken its shape from the community and in return the community has been shaped by the school. By advancing a student's notion of place and community, this school takes the responsibility of an educational facility beyond what is normally perceived.

Community response has been extremely positive and feedback gained from post-occupancy reviews with school staff and committee members serves as verification that the design met the primary needs.

General project timeframe from start to finish was approximately three years.

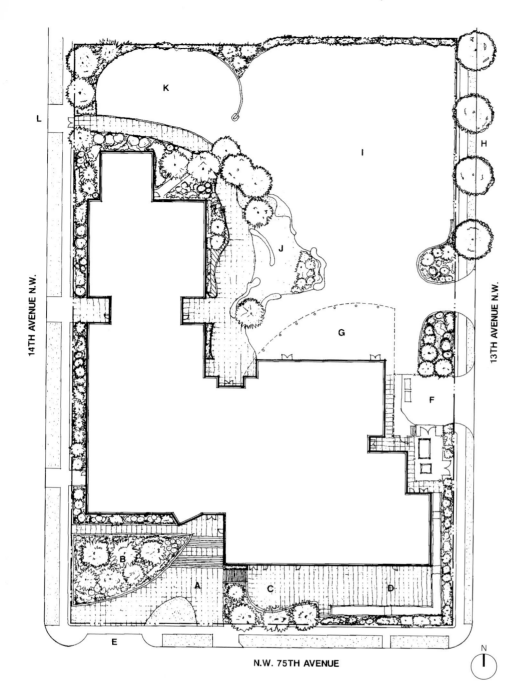

ARCHITECT
DLR Group

TYPE OF FACILITY
Elementary School

TYPE OF CONSTRUCTION
New

SITE AREA
2.7 acres

BUILDING AREA
65,500 square feet

CONSTUCTION COST
$9.1 M

STATUS OF PROJECT
Completed 1999

NUMBER OF STUDENTS
500

STRUCTURAL ENGINEER
Symonds Consulting Engineers

MECHANICAL/ELECTRICAL ENGINEER
DLR Group

CONTRACTOR
WICK Constructors

A Entry plaza
B Butterfly garden
C Environmental learning
D Child care plan
E Drop-off
F Service
G Covered play
H Bus loading
I Hard-surface play
J Soft-surface play
K Play structure
L Drop-off

14TH AVENUE N.W.

13TH AVENUE N.W.

N.W. 75TH AVENUE

N

WYCALLIS ELEMENTARY

ARCHITECT'S STATEMENT

Twenty-two classrooms, library, gymnasium, administration, cafeteria, and separate district offices in the same facility.

Mechanical process

The process could best be described as a circle. The School Board acted as the final approving entity. The superintendent set the overall goals of the district and reviewed the teachers' 'wish lists' after the interview process. The principal acted as a liaison between the teachers and the superintendent. The superintendent reviewed the teachers' needs or 'perceived' needs with the architect. A final determination was made and presented to the school board for final approval in a public meeting.

Design conceptual process

Toys 'R' Us Story. The method used to meet the primal needs of the client was done by placing ourselves in a child's mind for a day. This ultimately led to the Toys 'R' Us trip. This event engaged the design team in innovative solutions that would make this project a 'special place' for kids to learn. The design team was given a budget of $5.00 and asked to pick out an item(s) that best represented the team's concept of a place to learn. This item would remain in their station as a reference until the completion of the project. After the items were selected, the team was whisked to the McDonald's to eat kid's food and observe the play area. After a short discussion, the team, along with their takeout food, were taken to the site. The burgers, fries, and cokes were eaten on the empty site with a discussion of what kids like and how to integrate these likes into the learning environment and built form … colors, giants, candy, games, rocks, pets, toys,

computers … this day was to set the pace for the duration of the project. Always dreaming, always experimenting — searching for the best possible solution.

The end result

The end result of the process was the overlaying of the design/conceptual process on top of the mechanical process and program requirements.

ARCHITECT
Quad Three Group, Inc.

TYPE OF FACILITY
Elementary School

TYPE OF CONSTRUCTION
New

SITE AREA
5.75 acres

BUILDING AREA
61,520 square feet

TOTAL PROJECT COST
$9,010,617

STATUS OF PROJECT
Completed 1999

NUMBER OF STUDENTS
500

**STRUCTURAL/MECHANICAL/
ELECTRICAL ENGINEER**
Quad Three Group, Inc.

1 Lobby
2 Library
3 Outdoor classroom
4 Gymnasium
5 Kindergarten wing
6 Administration
7 Classroom block
8 Secondary lobby
9 District administration
10 Mechanical
11 Cafeteria
12 Band room
13 Art room
14 Computer room
15 Butterfly garden
16 Planting garden

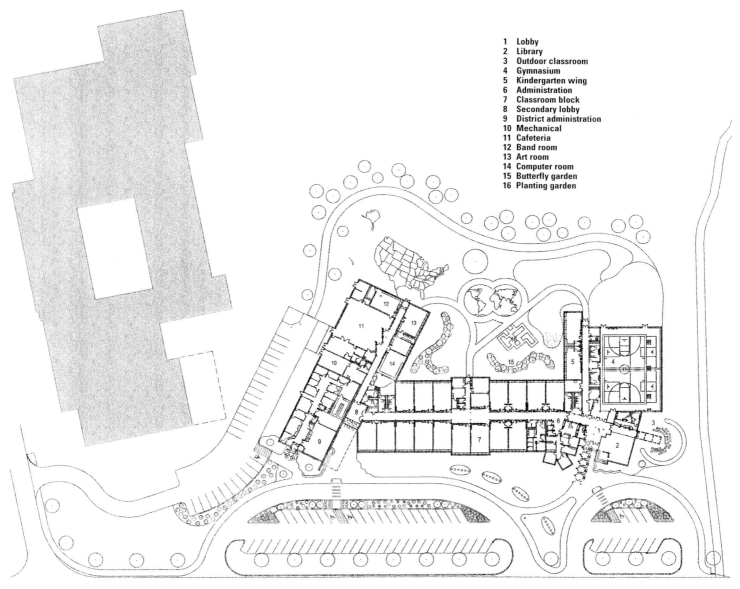

EDUCATIONAL FACILITIES

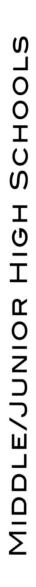

MIDDLE/JUNIOR HIGH SCHOOLS

Discovery Middle School

ARCHITECT'S STATEMENT

In designing this middle school, the challenge was to accommodate 900 students in a future-oriented facility that fits the steeply sloped, forested site while relating to the neighborhood. The solution was to build a three-story brick veneer structure depressed one level below grade. Planning began with a symposium involving nearly 70 people. The collaborative design process helped the architects create innovative spaces to support the educational needs of today's and tomorrow's students.

The school's villages consist of flexible classrooms for team teaching. Plazas, or cooperative learning areas for project-based work, serve each village. A unique distributed media program delivers electronic and printed materials directly to students. The loft is a comfortable area for reading. A large open space called the tool box is divided into five zones: a research center, wet/dry lab, art design, technology education, and fabrication. This area has outdoor access for environmental studies. Other features include a gallery for exhibits; a forum or town square; a community center for parents and school partners; and a wellness center to promote lifetime health and fitness.

ARCHITECT
LSW Architects, P.C.

TYPE OF FACILITY
Middle/Junior High School

TYPE OF CONSTRUCTION
New

SITE AREA
22.38 acres

BUILDING AREA
124,870 square feet

TOTAL PROJECT COST
$14,050,716

STATUS OF PROJECT
Completed 1995

NUMBER OF STUDENTS
900

STRUCTURAL ENGINEER
Kramer Gehlen Associates

MECHANICAL ENGINEER
Manfull-Curtis Inc.

ELECTRICAL ENGINEER
MKE & Associates, Inc.

CONTRACTOR
Absher Construction

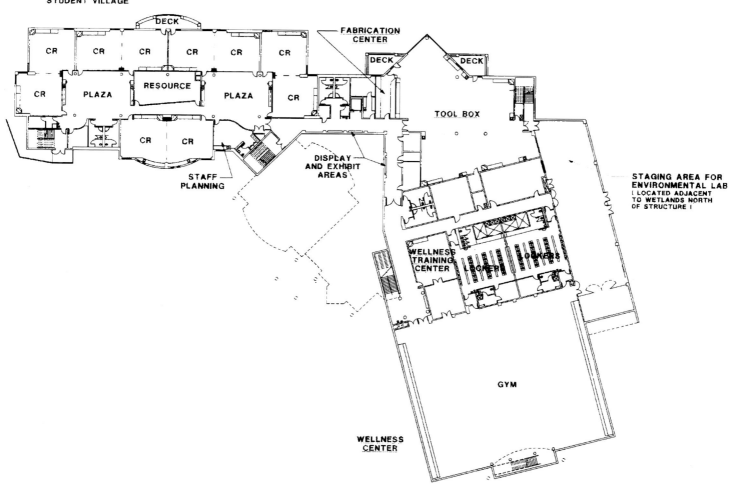

HORACE MANN SCHOOL

CITATION

RIVERDALE, NEW YORK

ARCHITECT'S STATEMENT

The architect's challenge was to create a master plan for an independent school's bucolic site near Manhattan, providing a new home for 390 middle school children, highlighting the arts, and unifying the architecture of the 11.5 acre campus.

The new middle school environment brings identity to the often neglected children in grades six, seven, and eight. The children's spaces are organized on three levels overlooking a commons room. Classrooms are clustered around a teaching center on each floor. The children share a circulation space furnished with display cases, bulletin boards, and window seats overlooking the commons area. Rooms are designed with corner bay windows, which allow children to work close to their natural environment while enjoying state-of-the-art technology.

In the new arts/dining building, a two-story entry gallery allows art to be viewed from the far reaches of the campus. Circulation through the 'route of the arts,' a generous stair cascading down the edge of the building, engages all members of the school community with the arts as they travel past painting, sculpture, ceramics, photography, printmaking, orchestral, choral, and gallery spaces to their destinations.

A clock tower punctuates the corner of the quadrangle and neo-gothic elements from the existing structures are integrated into a cohesive new architectural vocabulary for the campus.

ARCHITECT
**Gruzen Samton Architects
Planners & Interior Designers
LLP**

TYPE OF FACILITY
**Middle/Junior High School / High
School / Master Plan**

TYPE OF CONSTRUCTION
New/Addition/Renovation

NUMBER OF STUDENTS
990

SITE AREA
11.5 acres

BUILDING AREA
130,000 square feet

TOTAL PROJECT COST
$33 M

STATUS OF PROJECT
Completed August 1999

STRUCTURAL ENGINEER
Severud Associates

MECHANICAL ENGINEER
Syska & Hennessy, Inc.

CONTRACTOR
Lehrer McGovern Bovis, Inc.

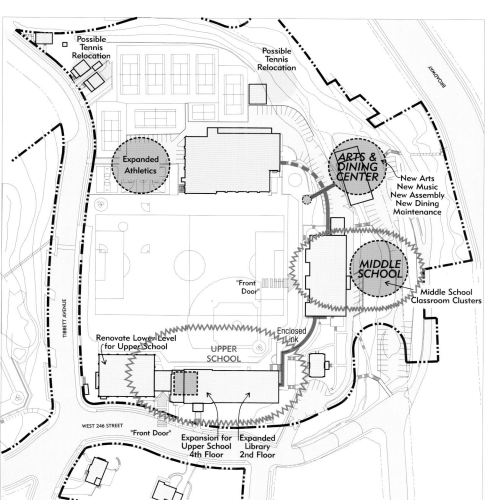

KEY

Existing Building

New Construction

School Core Areas

0   50   100ft

N

BEDFORD MIDDLE SCHOOL

ARCHITECT'S STATEMENT

Collaboration between architects, educators, and the public during the design process has resulted in a new middle school to support a community of shared learners. Discussions with educators revealed that despite the earlier adoption of a team approach to learning, teachers in specialty areas such as art and music felt that existing schools isolated them from the team's daily life. To address this, a central commons was developed to provide a focus for all members of the school community. This plan brings all subject and support areas together—academic teams, art, music, athletics, and administration—encouraging the spontaneous exploration

of ideas. The commons itself contains the media center, cafeteria, and an outdoor courtyard, all designed to allow students choices of activity as they move through the day. Each team is self-contained with a collaboration area linking the science labs, classrooms, and bathrooms. This area is linked vertically with the team below and contains large windows to make learning an enjoyable experience. Teams are then grouped into learning communities and share resource and team rooms.

ARCHITECT
Jeter, Cook & Jepson Architects, Inc.

TYPE OF FACILITY
Middle/Junior High School

TYPE OF CONSTRUCTION
New

SITE AREA
100 acres

BUILDING AREA
197,000 square feet

TOTAL PROJECT COST
$40 M

STATUS OF PROJECT
Completed August 2001

NUMBER OF STUDENTS
800

STRUCTURAL ENGINEER
BVH Engineers

MECHANICAL/ELECTRICAL ENGINEER
H.P. Engineering

CONTRACTOR
Turner Construction

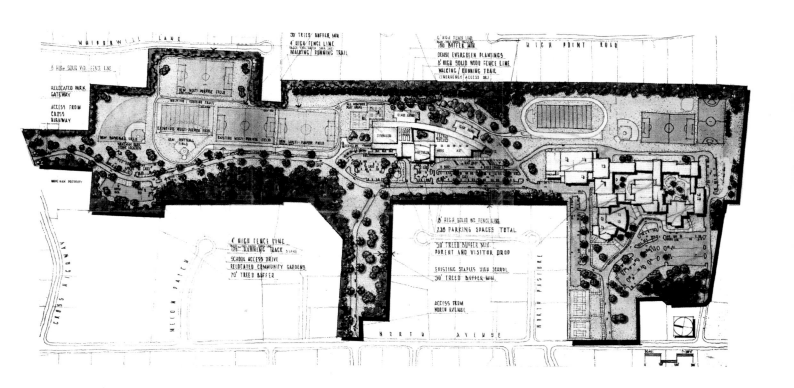

CENTENNIAL CAMPUS MAGNET MIDDLE SCHOOL

RALEIGH, NORTH CAROLINA

ARCHITECT'S STATEMENT

The idea for an exemplary middle school with an affiliated teacher development center, developed collaboratively in the school system and the university, emerged in 1988 from discussions with the local council of governments. During the next two years, a planning committee was established. Aided by a small planning grant, the committee was charged with developing an educational program and governance agreement for the school and the teacher development/outreach program.

The program was developed to address the critical development issues facing middle school students. The learning experience required in middle school will play a strong role in shaping a student's future. The middle school/research and development center were designed to meet this

challenge by providing an exemplary educational community of young adolescents and adults who learn by actively discovering, integrating, and applying knowledge in a dynamic global and technological environment. The curriculum has been designed to emphasize hands-on, active learning techniques, and will be highly interactive with adults through the university's involvement, and through internships, group studies, and community service projects. The architecture of the facility will involve these interactions with group meeting rooms, project rooms, and shared resources at the teacher outreach center.

ARCHITECT
Boney Architects, Inc.

TYPE OF FACILITY
**Middle/Junior High School /
Innovative Learning Environment**

TYPE OF CONSTRUCTION
New

SITE AREA
17 acres

BUILDING AREA
132,000 square feet

TOTAL PROJECT COST
$14,170,000

STATUS OF PROJECT
Completed April 2000

NUMBER OF STUDENTS
600

STRUCTURAL ENGINEER
Morrison & Sullivan Engineers

MECHANICAL ENGINEER
Cheatham & Associates

ELECTRICAL ENGINEER
Dewberry & Davis

CONTRACTOR
D. H. Griffin

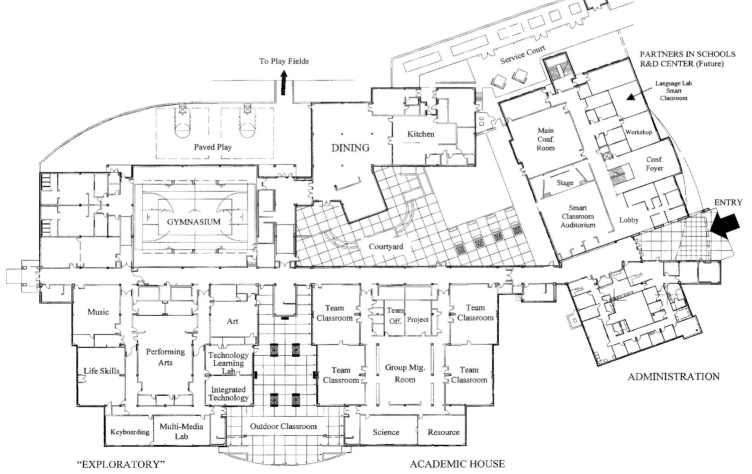

To Play Fields

PARTNERS IN SCHOOLS
R&D CENTER (Future)

Service Court

Language Lab
Smart Classroom

Paved Play

DINING

Kitchen

Main Conf. Room

Workshop

Conf. Foyer

Stage

Smart Classroom Auditorium

Lobby

ENTRY

GYMNASIUM

Courtyard

Music

Art

Team Classroom

Team Off.

Project

Team Classroom

ADMINISTRATION

Life Skills

Performing Arts

Technology Learning Lab

Team Classroom

Group Mtg. Room

Team Classroom

Integrated Technology

Keyboarding

Multi-Media Lab

Outdoor Classroom

Science

Resource

"EXPLORATORY"

ACADEMIC HOUSE

DERBY MIDDLE SCHOOL

BIRMINGHAM, MICHIGAN

ARCHITECT'S STATEMENT

Prominently located at the new 'front door' of the existing middle school, the new Interactive Tech Center features a gently curving façade that encloses two major activity areas. Upon entering, a generous two- and three-dimensional display space is provided to exhibit exciting student projects. Special lighting, floor, and ceiling finishes are incorporated to reinforce this image.

The design of this project responds to several major objectives:

- Provide a stimulating, flexible environment to reinforce the District's commitment to integrated learning in technology, math, and science.
- Provide a facility that fosters teaming.
- Stress interactive use of emerging technology both as a design and simulation tool.

- Provide two distinct areas to facilitate design/research and actual hands-on prototype fabrication.
- Create a facility which is the 'symbolic focus' of integrated curriculum at the school.

Flexible lab areas include movable work centers supported with the proper utility services to facilitate a variety of exploration. A central work area for faculty commands a dramatic view of the entire teaching space. Student project storage space and other support areas provide a comprehensive facility. High ceilings flooded with controlled, glare-free natural light provide an upbeat, stimulating interior environment. Contiuous new classroom instructional areas provide the opportunity for group interdisciplinary curriculum to occur.

ARCHITECT
TMP Associates, Inc.

TYPE OF FACILITY
Middle/Junior High School / Innovative Learning Environment

TYPE OF CONSTRUCTION
Addition/Renovation

NUMBER OF STUDENTS
800

BUILDING AREA
122,200 square feet (existing); 14,640 square feet (new)

TOTAL PROJECT COST
$5,714,874

STATUS OF PROJECT
Completed August 1995

STRUCTURAL ENGINEER
TMP Associates, Inc.

MECHANICAL/ELECTRICAL ENGINEER
Giffels Hoyem Basso Associates, Inc.

CONTRACTOR
Barton Malow

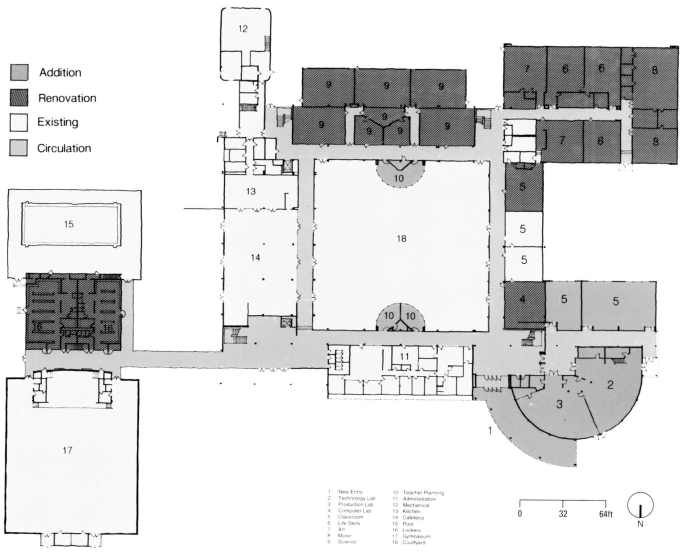

Addition
Renovation
Existing
Circulation

1   New Entry
2   Technology Lab
3   Production Lab
4   Computer Lab
5   Classroom
6   Life Skills
7   Art
8   Music
9   Science
10 Teacher Planning
11 Administration
12 Mechanical
13 Kitchen
14 Cafeteria
15 Pool
16 Lockers
17 Gymnasium
18 Courtyard

0   32   64ft

N

JAMES MADISON SCHOOL OF EXCELLENCE

ARCHITECT'S STATEMENT

This middle school serves two functions: a replacement facility for 1,000 students and a comprehensive community resource, the result of a highly inclusive and collaborative process that solicited and incorporated commentary from multiple constituents—city, administration, community groups, building committees, and a public/private partnership newly formed to launch the center—over a six-month planning and design timeframe.

There were three key objectives:

- project an inviting image within an inner city community, creating an enduring symbol of commitment, continuity, and renewal

- integrate community and adult education usage without compromising security, efficiency, or academic mission

- retain the scale and intimacy characteristic of smaller facilities, ensuring students a progressive, yet personalized learning environment.

In response, the building functions as a 'student village,' with a commons, main street, and neighborhoods—each functional area a distinct building block linked by the primary circulation path. Classroom blocks are further subdivided into four individual houses of 250 students creating a school within a school. The student street is traveled by all daily, fostering interaction among users and animation of the space.

Zoned separately, yet sharing facilities, the community center functions as a hub for social services, provides remedial and continuing education, and organizes recreational and sports activities.

ARCHITECT
Cannon Design

TYPE OF FACILITY
**Middle High School /
Innovative Learning Environment**

TYPE OF CONSTRUCTION
New

SITE AREA
15.7 acres

NUMBER OF STUDENTS
1,000

TOTAL PROJECT COST
$32,280,000

STATUS OF PROJECT
Completed September 1998

STRUCTURAL/MECHANICAL/
ELECTRICAL ENGINEER
Cannon Design

CONTRACTOR
LeChase Construction

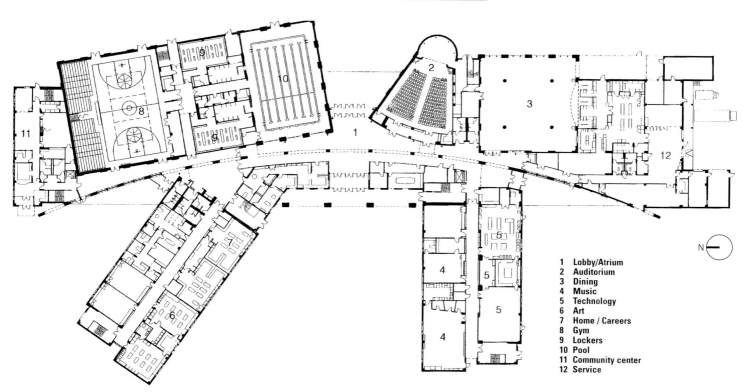

1 Lobby/Atrium
2 Auditorium
3 Dining
4 Music
5 Technology
6 Art
7 Home / Careers
8 Gym
9 Lockers
10 Pool
11 Community center
12 Service

N

MIDDLE/JUNIOR HIGH SCHOOLS

KAPOLEI MIDDLE SCHOOL

KAPOLEI, OAHU, HAWAII

ARCHITECT'S STATEMENT

The design of Kapolei Middle School was shaped by use of a design charette process with representatives from a 38-member community taskforce, a 12-member steering committee, an 18-member teacher ad hoc curriculum committee, and 600 student representatives, working in conjunction with the architects.

Focusing on the needs of middle school students and rethinking how they learn has resulted in a totally different kind of school for Hawaii. The end results were:

a Recognizing that educational philosophies have changed and will continue to evolve, dynamic flexibility has been incorporated into the classroom design.

b Understanding the needs of middle school students, a nurturing and caring environment with safe and comfortable places to gather has been incorporated into the design.

c The impact of technology has been incorporated with linkages to the community and innovative learning centers.

d Realizing the importance of culture in preparing students for the future, cultural concepts have been incorporated with the use of performance hula mounds, gathering courtyards and gardens in each 'house,' and outdoor performance amphitheaters.

e Valuing lifelong learning, and the wealth of knowledge and experiences in the workplace and community, opportunities for networking and sharing of resources have been defined.

f Above all, the design efforts and accomplishments of parents, teachers, students, and the community have generated an unprecedented sense of ownership and pride in the school.

A true 'New Century School' and an 'Island School for the Future' has been established.

ARCHITECT
Mitsunaga & Associates, Inc.

TYPE OF FACILITY
Middle/Junior High School

TYPE OF CONSTRUCTION
New

SITE AREA
20 acres

BUILDING AREA
151,477 square feet

TOTAL PROJECT COST
$38 M

STATUS OF PROJECT
Completed May 1999

NUMBER OF STUDENTS
1,200–1,500

STRUCTURAL ENGINEER
Mitsunaga & Associates, Inc.

MECHANICAL ENGINEER
Thermal Engineering Corporation

ELECTRICAL ENGINEER
ECS, Inc.

CONTRACTOR
Albert C. Kobayashi Inc.

ROOF

SIDE ELEVATION

SECTION

COURTYARD ELEVATION

MIAMI EDISON MIDDLE SCHOOL

ARCHITECT'S STATEMENT

The design transformed an old architectural relic to its original grandeur and updated its educational function for the needs of the 21st century. The cohesiveness of the design links the student to a new educational process at every juncture. That is, a new 'concept school,' embodied in multi-use, state-of-the-art, technologically equipped classrooms, a media center, technology laboratory, group workstations, and computer labs—all of which can evolve as the demands of education and technology become more complex.

The client's primary needs follow:

- Preserve and restore the architecturally and historically significant portions of the existing facility.

- Within the historic context, create a school for the 21st century that bridges the gap between the inside and outside world of the classroom; a learning milieu that redefines America's traditional educational environment.

The process to define the design and verify that it met the needs of the school involved numerous discussions and group meetings with the school board, politicians, alumni, teachers, and students. The resulting design speaks to the adaptability of the historic structures to accommodate modern educational facility program requirements. The final result is proof that good design and historic preservation can enhance the lives of both students and faculty, and return a sense of place and pride to the community.

The combination of new and historic structure creates an architectural richness that links the past to the future.

ARCHITECT
R. J. Heisenbottle Architects, PA

TYPE OF FACILITY
Middle/Junior High School

TYPE OF CONSTRUCTION
New/Renovation

SITE AREA
14.5 acres

BUILDING AREA
203,000 square feet

TOTAL PROJECT COST
$37,389,617

STATUS OF PROJECT
Completed January 1997

NUMBER OF STUDENTS
1,475

STRUCTURAL ENGINEER
Balsara Fonticello & Associates

MECHANICAL ENGINEER
Lagomasino & Associates, PA

ELECTRICAL ENGINEER
Vital Engineering, PA

CONTRACTOR
TAP/3D International

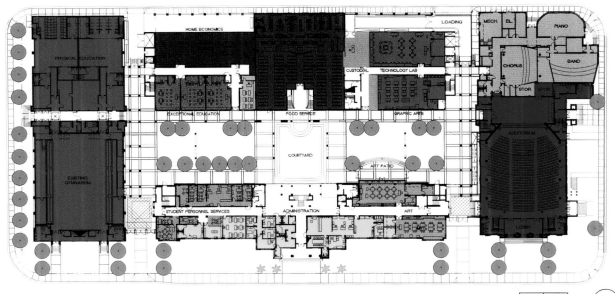

MIDDLE/JUNIOR HIGH SCHOOLS

PLEASANT RIDGE MIDDLE SCHOOL

STILWELL, KANSAS

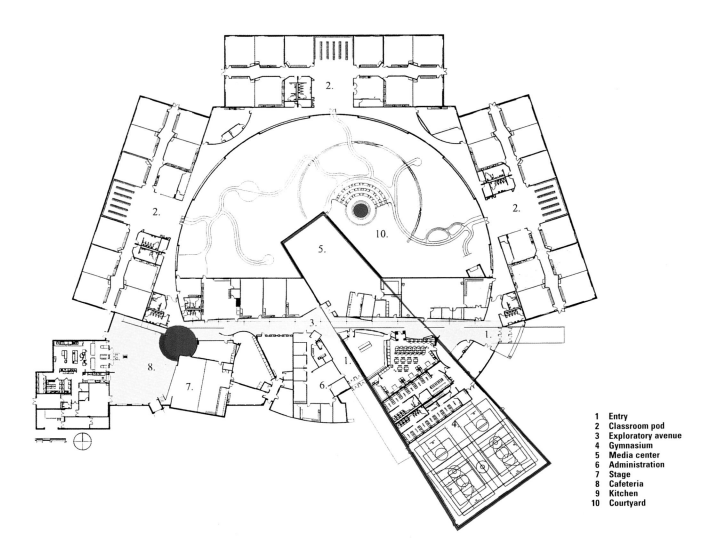

1   Entry
2   Classroom pod
3   Exploratory avenue
4   Gymnasium
5   Media center
6   Administration
7   Stage
8   Cafeteria
9   Kitchen
10   Courtyard

ARCHITECT'S STATEMENT

A new middle school developed for a fast-growing community, this facility was designed to embrace and enhance the middle school experience. The building order was conceived to promote the idea of exploration—a core concept of middle-level educational philosophy.

A semi-circular courtyard, visible from interior circulation areas, serves as a visual orientation tool; it is flanked by each of the three independent wings of the school (one for each grade). These are divided into two teams each, allowing for small learning groups in this large school. Spaces are flexible, allowing for team teaching when appropriate.

The exploratory curriculum areas, such as Art, Music, Family and Consumer Sciences, Industrial Technology, Physical Education, and World Languages, are grouped along a prominent entry corridor. The placement of these is intended both to allow cross-circular interaction and to elevate the importance and visibility of the instructional programs. Striking forms, carefully selected materials, and the artful use of light give special character to this 'Exploratory Avenue' and to celebrate the uniqueness of each of the curriculum areas housed there.

ARCHITECT
Gould Evans Affiliates

TYPE OF FACILITY
Middle/Junior High School

TYPE OF CONSTRUCTION
New

SITE AREA
36 acres

BUILDING AREA
119,400 square feet

TOTAL PROJECT COST
$15.4 M

NUMBER OF STUDENTS
750

STATUS OF PROJECT
Completed 1997

STRUCTURAL ENGINEER
Bob D. Campbell & Company

MECHANICAL/ELECTRICAL
ENGINEER
Larson-Binkley Associates, Inc.

CONTRACTOR
J. E. Dunn Construction Co.

RANCHO DEL REY MIDDLE SCHOOL

CHULKA VISTA, CALIFORNIA

ARCHITECT'S STATEMENT

Over a six-month period, the Community Team confirmed a number of key principles, which have guided the programming and design, namely:

- An interdisciplinary approach to education.

- Focus on technology and communications.

- Development of societal skills.

- Empowered student: self-esteem, mentoring, major student project, community service.

Each site configuration was evaluated by the team and rated based on such functional criteria as: traffic and parking, deliveries, construction, in addition to views, breezes, open space, on-campus circulation, surveillance, security, and so on.

The typical cluster of eight classrooms, for 200–240 students, is arranged to form an 'academic courtyard' and a 'portfolio patio.'

The design parti relates to an 'open landscape arrangement' of courtyards, patios, lawns, and promenades, which enhance the educational setting of the various buildings on the campus.

The architectural details for each cluster, as well as its associated hardscape, are specific to its educational subject matter. Likewise, the architectural image/theme for the non-classroom buildings is 'village buildings,' while the media-library has its image/theme of reading 'in an arboretum' and 'under the stars.'

ARCHITECT
Martinez + Cutri

TYPE OF FACILITY
Middle/Junior High School

TYPE OF CONSTRUCTION
New

SITE AREA
25 acres

BUILDING AREA
136,300 square feet

TOTAL PROJECT COST
$30,361,200

STATUS OF PROJECT
Completed January 1999

NUMBER OF STUDENTS
1,400

STRUCTURAL ENGINEER
Burkett & Wong Engineers

MECHANICAL/ELECTRICAL
ENGINEER
T K & G

CONTRACTOR
Taylor-Ball

TIMBERCREST JUNIOR HIGH SCHOOL

ARCHITECT'S STATEMENT

The original program for the school was based on a department curriculum model.

During early discussions with district administrators, the design team modified the program to reflect the 'neighborhood' delivery model, which was just coming into use in the district. Working with educators over a three-month period, the architects created a new physical program to accommodate junior high instruction.

The design team created a central shared space in each neighborhood. The client required that the shared space be visible from surrounding classrooms but not a circulation path to them. The resulting

design carefully arranges classrooms and exterior doors to the courtyard to accomplish this goal.

Another key requirement of the project was making the exterior environment more accessible to the students. The design team created a central courtyard to respond to this. The courtyard, landscaped to recall a stream on the site, provides a passageway between buildings, an outdoor commons, an educational area, and a performance area in the heart of the campus.

1 Environmental educational trail
2 Wetlands
3 Retention ponds
4 All purpose sports field
5 Tennis
6 Track/Football
7 Courtyard

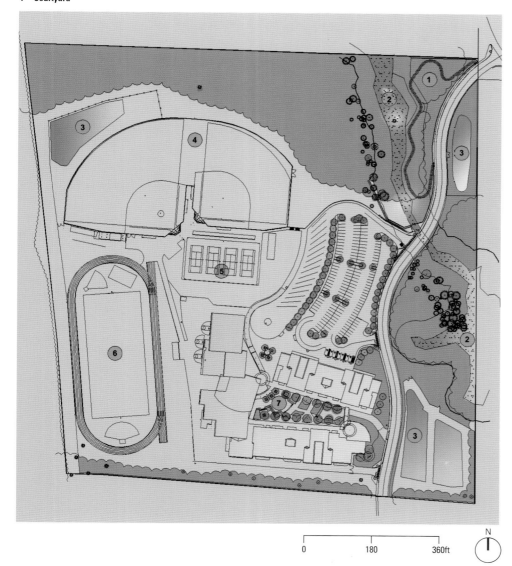

0   180   360ft

N

ARCHITECT
Northwest Architectural Company

TYPE OF FACILITY
Middle/Junior High School

TYPE OF CONSTRUCTION
New

NUMBER OF STUDENTS
900

SITE AREA
35 acres

BUILDING AREA
104,000 square feet

TOTAL PROJECT COST
$16.2 M

STATUS OF PROJECT
Completed September 1997

STRUCTURAL ENGINEER
Coughlin, Porter, Lundeen

MECHANICAL/ELECTRICAL
ENGINEER
Hargis Engineers

CONTRACTOR
Berschauer Phillips

Veterans Park Schools

Architect's statement

An energetic and creative process of interactive design was used to define the program of spaces for these schools. A committee of 35 teachers, administrators, facility planners, maintenance staff, and members of the community brainstormed in a workshop during the spring of 1998. The resulting program of spaces suggested the following priorities:

- The building must provide a flexible environment for learning, space to facilitate traditional modes of instruction, and enable the shift to more dynamic self-guided learning styles. To accomplish this, a variety of large and small spaces must be provided.

- To facilitate increasing levels of community involvement with the school, special considerations must be made to allow individuals and groups such as

mentors/tutors, specialists, parents, and community leaders to use the facilities.

- Technology must be integrated in all aspects of the school environment. The use of computers, multimedia presentations, and distance learning programs are needed to prepare children for the future.

- School leaders must promote positive social interactions among students, faculty, and the community as a whole.

The process included follow-up meetings with the committee members during the design phase.

ARCHITECT
Boney Architects, Inc.

TYPE OF FACILITY
Middle/Junior High School / High School

TYPE OF CONSTRUCTION
New

SITE AREA
212 acres

BUILDING AREA
390,580 square feet

STATUS OF PROJECT
Completed 2001

NUMBER OF STUDENTS
2,400

STRUCTURAL ENGINEER
Morrison & Sullivan Engineers

MECHANICAL ENGINEER
Cheatham & Associates Engineers

ELECTRICAL ENGINEER
Dewberry & Davis Engineers

WINDSOR MIDDLE SCHOOL

WINDSOR, CALIFORNIA

ARCHITECT'S STATEMENT

The Windsor Middle School is unique in the way the architects used a participatory design process to bring the diverse needs and wishes of the citizens of this new small town to consensus on a strong design statement. Parents, town leaders, and neighbors were continually involved in the design process.

This suburban community has its roots as a farming community and the main buildings reflect the agricultural vocabulary of the area.

The special social and academic needs of a middle school are addressed by organizing the classrooms into three independent clusters, each around a courtyard. Each cluster has science and art labs as well as teacher work rooms and all support facilities. This provides for flexibility in organizing the school in different ways.

The library/media center is the hub of the communications networks for this state-of-the-art technology school to accommodate the new curriculum requirements. All three classroom clusters are organized around this building making it the focus of the academic portion of the campus.

The campus is organized along two strong allees of ornamental shade trees that unify the campus and organize the exterior circulation.

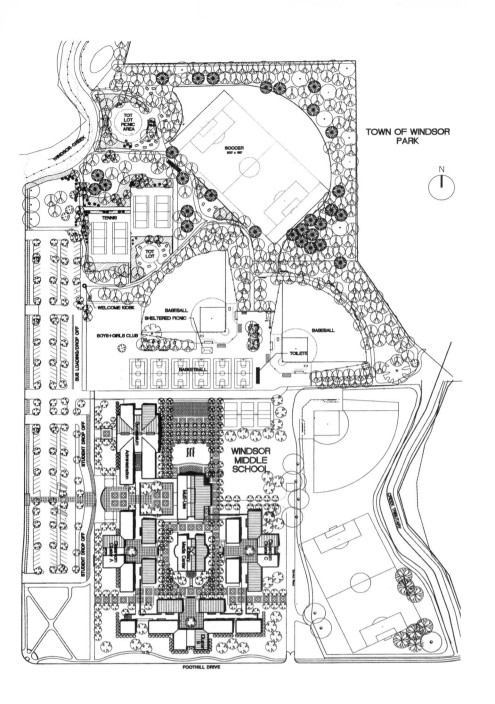

ARCHITECT
Quattrocchi Kwok Architects

ASSOCIATE ARCHITECT
**Marquis Associates of
San Francisco**

TYPE OF FACILITY
Middle/Junior High School

TYPE OF CONSTRUCTION
New

SITE AREA
12.3 acres

BUILDING AREA
67,200 square feet

TOTAL PROJECT COST
$14.5 M

STATUS OF PROJECT
Completed 1997

NUMBER OF STUDENTS
750

STRUCTURAL ENGINEER
**Structural Engineers
Collaborative**

MECHANICAL ENGINEER
Horn Engineers

ELECTRICAL ENGINEER
Myers Engineering Group

EDUCATIONAL FACILITIES

HIGH SCHOOLS

MANASSAS PARK HIGH SCHOOL

ARCHITECT'S STATEMENT

Recently opened, Manassas Park High School represents a comprehensive reinvention of local public education. The new school supplements the former high school on site—now the city's intermediate school—to create an academic campus that serves as a civic focal point for the community. With the building of the new high school, the school board hoped to transform the educational atmosphere into a source of inspiration and pride. The new three-story building accommodates 650 students; a future classroom addition will increase capacity to 800 students.

Half the site is densely wooded and slopes to an attractive creek bed. The front of the property, however, is bounded by an industrial park. A new screen of maple trees along the access road will create a cloistered campus for the two schools and shelter the grounds from the busy road and nearby industry. A gap in this screen opens to a front lawn and bus loop. Both academic and gymnasium entrances front the green space, as would an addition to the intermediate school called for in a campus master plan. The new building forms a fairly dense, L-shaped street wall so that most public spaces focus their views toward the wooded part of the site, away from the road. A primary circulation corridor ties together the athletic and academic buildings and sets up a link to a future intermediate school courtyard and fields beyond.

The building's central drum is nestled behind the classroom wings and contains the school's main gathering places. Clerestory windows fill this rotunda with natural light, allowing the wooded landscape to become a constant reference. Administrative and food service spaces, as well as the music and art programs, occupy the lower floor. They surround a stepped ground-floor commons that can accommodate both student dining and various forms of assembly—augmenting a conventional cafeteria with a versatile, all-school theater space. The open upper floor of the drum is ringed by the media center with views through the commons and to the outdoors.

The school's public spaces activate the ground floor, while the classrooms and labs are removed to the upper two floors. The classrooms are gathered around four teacher resource areas, centered on light-filled stair halls that serve as informal meeting and presentation areas. These halls focus the shuffle of typical corridors into usable space—the stairs themselves double as seating, providing places for intimate groups of teachers and students.

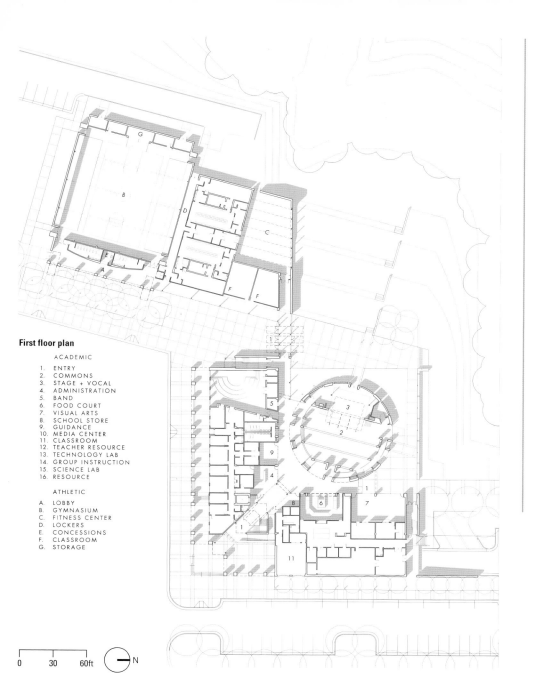

First floor plan

ACADEMIC

1. ENTRY
2. COMMONS
3. STAGE + VOCAL
4. ADMINISTRATION
5. BAND
6. FOOD COURT
7. VISUAL ARTS
8. SCHOOL STORE
9. GUIDANCE
10. MEDIA CENTER
11. CLASSROOM
12. TEACHER RESOURCE
13. TECHNOLOGY LAB
14. GROUP INSTRUCTION
15. SCIENCE LAB
16. RESOURCE

ATHLETIC

A. LOBBY
B. GYMNASIUM
C. FITNESS CENTER
D. LOCKERS
E. CONCESSIONS
F. CLASSROOM
G. STORAGE

0   30   60ft   N

ARCHITECT
VMDO Architects, PC

TYPE OF FACILITY
High School

TYPE OF CONSTRUCTION
New

SITE AREA
59.6 acres

BUILDING AREA
102,000 square feet

TOTAL PROJECT COST
$14 M

STATUS OF PROJECT
Completed January 1999

NUMBER OF STUDENTS
650

STRUCTURAL ENGINEER
Fox & Associates

MECHANICAL/ELECTRICAL/
PLUMBING ENGINEERS
2rw Consulting Engineers

CIVIL ENGINEER
Barnes & Johnson, Inc., Civil Engineers

CONTRACTOR
SPN Construction Management

The academic spaces can be used in various combinations—each of the four sections can be treated as a distinct academy within the school or paired vertically as two independent houses, reducing the scale of a consolidated high school. Flexibility allows teachers to work together toward integrated curricula and structure both their classes and rooms to support inventive teaching strategies.

KENT ISLAND HIGH SCHOOL

STEVENSVILLE, MARYLAND

ARCHITECT'S STATEMENT

Kent Island High School is a 1,200-student, technology-based school that is located along the Chesapeake Bay on the Eastern Shore of Maryland. The major concern addressed by the planning committee centered around creating a facility that becomes a focal point on Kent Island where both the students and the community feel a sense of identity and belonging. The planning process for Kent Island High School provided a unique forum for community, civic, and business leaders, teachers, staff, students, and architects to learn from each other and become partners to accomplish a unified goal. In the end, the resulting school and design program provided customized, imaginative solutions to school and community goals and objectives.

The site entry is flanked by ponds and wetlands to emphasize the island nature of

the region and to provide an environmental study area for instruction. The architectural language, expressed by exposed structural steel frame construction and detailing, reflects the nautical character of the Eastern Shore Region.

The development and refinement of a student main street and an interdisciplinary program cluster concept are vehicles which create a sense of community within the entire school. The building plan is organized around a central main street that creates a student and community gathering place. The instructional areas intersect main street with a core circulation loop at an open-air stair. Academic/career-oriented clusters are grouped to encourage relationships between classes and disciplines, and to foster personal growth.

ARCHITECT
Grimm and Parker Architects

TYPE OF FACILITY
High School

TYPE OF CONSTRUCTION
New

SITE AREA
46 acres

BUILDING AREA
189.785 square feet

TOTAL PROJECT COST
$19,494,111

STATUS OF PROJECT
Completed August 1998

NUMBER OF STUDENTS
1,200

STRUCTURAL ENGINEER
Wolfman and Associates

MECHANICAL/ELECTRICAL
ENGINEER
D. Brooks Cross, Chtd.

CONTRACTOR
Donohoe Construction Company

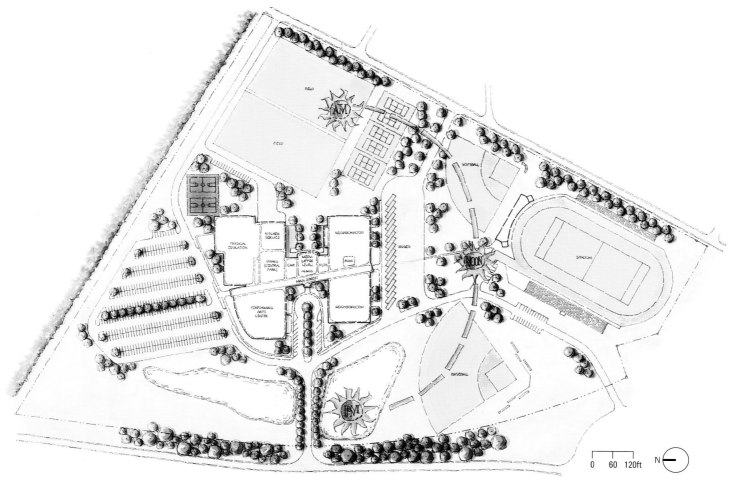

HIGH SCHOOLS

BERKELEY HIGH SCHOOL, BUILDINGS G AND H

ARCHITECT'S STATEMENT

Throughout the two-month programming and design phase, the design team was very sensitive to the historic significance of the site as well as the needs of a high school in the 21st century. Extensive workshops were held with the faculty, the department chairs, the administration, the community historical preservation society, the district staff, and the school board to ensure the design team met the requirements of the educational program and the community while maintaining the historical character of the school. The design emphasizes the Art Deco style of the campus, increases usable square footage, improves supervision, and provides total ADA/Title 24 Accessibility, including elevators and ramps.

Buildings G and H underwent a complete seismic and structural upgrade to exceed current codes, which required gutting the entire inside of the structures for new walls and mechanical, plumbing, electrical, and communications systems. The buildings were restored to their original grandeur through an extensive exterior face-lift, including paint, glazing, site, and landscaping improvements. Through a post-occupancy analysis, the students and staff of Berkeley High School have expressed satisfaction with this new, state-of-the-art facility, which promotes learning and enhances community pride.

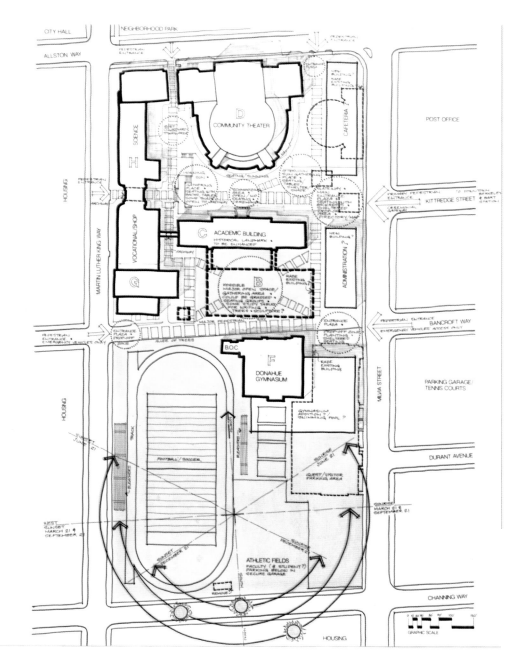

ARCHITECT
VBN Architects

ASSOCIATE ARCHITECT
WLC

TYPE OF FACILITY
High School

TYPE OF CONSTRUCTION
Renovation

SITE AREA
22 acres

BUILDING AREA
135,000 square feet

TOTAL PROJECT COST
$20 M

STATUS OF PROJECT
Completed 1997

NUMBER OF STUDENTS
3,000

STRUCTURAL ENGINEER
SOH & Associates Structural Engineer

MECHANICAL ENGINEERS
JYA Consulting Engineers

ELECTRICAL ENGINEER
T.H. Rogers Associates

CONTRACTOR
West Coast Contractor Inc.

BREWSTER ACADEMY
CLASSROOM/LIBRARY EXPANSION

WOLFEBORO, NEW HAMPSHIRE

ARCHITECT'S STATEMENT

The Learning Center is a unique collaborative between the architectural firm and the school design company. In 1994 the academy initiated a comprehensive re-engineering program using a School Design Model (SDM). The SDM is a comprehensive and technologically sophisticated program. The school provided the architect with highly articulated descriptions of the teaching practices and curriculum to be employed. The program incorporated the development of the classroom ergonomics design, teacher and student workspaces, and the ubiquitous use of technology through a 2000-port campus network.

The verification of the design process involved an interactive exchange of ideas. The primary concern of the project team was to adhere to the initial concepts of the SDM design criteria and to school wide concern for overall design integrity.

The beautiful lakeside campus provided both inspiration and discipline for the project. The architect's unique challenge was to design a 43,000 square foot addition and comprehensive renovation of 28,000 square feet that would reflect and enable the following teaching methodologies and practices:

- Adhere to educational standards and innovative technological requirements.
- Create a building with an aesthetic quality to match and enhance the beauty of the lakeside campus setting.
- Integrate the building's addition with the existing infrastructure—a 100-year-old New England-style school building.
- Design a space that would allow for individual curriculum for each learning cluster and in doing so provide the

teachers with the flexibility for interdisciplinary collaboration and planning.

The successful project integrates four teaching and learning clusters, four science lab/classroom suites, and a library learning center. Each architectural resolution in reference to project program reflects an educational design driver.

- The L-shaped classroom design and configuration of technology posts provide a backdrop in which different teaching practices can occur in a fully networked environment.
- The instructional support space is positioned at the core of the facility, increasing the interaction between teacher and learning disabled students while minimizing the stigma associated with pull-out programs.

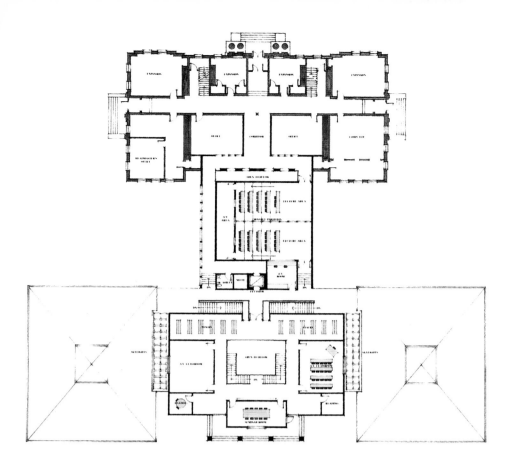

ARCHITECT
Spagnolo/Gisness & Associates, Inc.

TYPE OF FACILITY
High School / Alternative School / Innovative Learning Environment

TYPE OF CONSTRUCTION
Addition/Renovation

BUILDING AREA
70,000 square feet

TOTAL PROJECT COST
$2.5 M

STATUS OF PROJECT
Completed 1995

STRUCTURAL ENGINEER
Aberjona Engineering

CONTRACTOR
Gustafson Construction

- The integration of laboratory and instructional space enables science practicum to be more directly associated with lecture tutorial.

- The space promotes collaborative learning both directly and through the high bandwidth network.

- Collaborative learning space is reserved in the portion of the library learning center that provides the finest lake vistas.

The project is the beneficiary of a thoughtful orchestration of educational and architectural design principles at an uncommon level of precision and clarity.

CARMEL HIGH SCHOOL

ARCHITECT'S STATEMENT

As the initial step in master planning, the architect held planning sessions with members of the community and teachers, working together to define goals. Implementation of the master plan resulted in reorganization and expansion of the school to accommodate new educational needs and improve the school's image.

The new construction uses a continuous sky-lit street as an organizational element running the length of the school, knitting together existing spaces and additions and creating a sense of community. The street begins as a canopy next to the courtyard, where a two-story tower identifies the main entrance for students and visitors.

In front of the existing theater the street widens, forming a lobby for public performances. The street links student traffic from cross-corridors to the new media center, strategically placed at the hub to signify its importance to the school. The street ends at the expanded athletic complex, where the new student commons provides lunchtime seating or a lobby area for sports events.

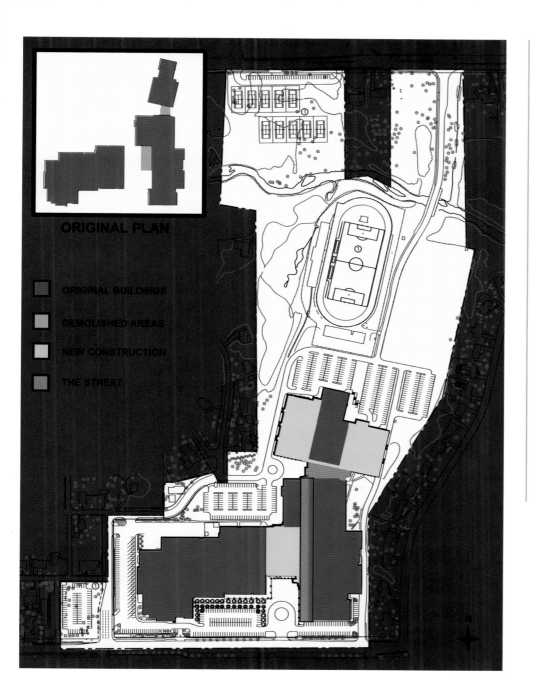

ORIGINAL PLAN

- ORIGINAL BUILDINGS
- DEMOLISHED AREAS
- NEW CONSTRUCTION
- THE STREET

ARCHITECT
Cripe & O'Donnell Architects and Engineers

TYPE OF FACILITY
High School

TYPE OF CONSTRUCTION
Addition/Renovation

SITE AREA
12.6 acres; 17.1 acres

BUILDING AREA
Renovation/Addition 547,301 square feet; total 742,862 square feet

TOTAL PROJECT COST
$49 M

STATUS OF PROJECT
Completed September 1998

NUMBER OF STUDENTS
3,600

STRUCTURAL ENGINEER
OWP&P

MECHANICAL/ELECTRICAL ENGINEER
Moore Engineering

CONTRACTOR
Huber, Hunt & Nicholas, Inc.

CENTENNIAL ACADEMIC AND ARTS CENTER, POMFRET SCHOOL

POMFRET, CONNECTICUT

ARCHITECT'S STATEMENT

This school is a highly regarded preparatory school offering rigorous academics, a substantial athletics program, and a special focus on the arts. 'Centennial Building'—celebrating the school's hundredth anniversary—was planned in response to recent growth to 300 students. The building would include art studios; carpentry, metal, and welding shops; 14 classrooms; and a 125-seat auditorium.

The design began in a series of interactive workshops in which faculty, students, staff, trustees, and alumni were asked about their dreams and needs. The workshops focused on the campus and site, the program, and the image of the building.

The campus plan, originally designed by Ernest Flagg, a well-known turn-of-the-century Beaux Arts architect, had been abandoned in recent campus development. Moving the historic Pyne Dormitory and

positioning the new Centennial Building on an axis with the original four-story School Building by Flagg, created an academic core at the center of the campus and re-established the principles of quadrangles and axes from Flagg's original plan.

The Centennial Building sits on a hill sloping to the west, which allows on-grade entry at two levels. At the lowest floor, the workshops and auditorium sit just off a campus road for easy access. The finishes are simple, with exposed ceilings. The auditorium doubles as a black box theater, with cable trays and a pipe grid for lighting.

The 14 classrooms and three seminar rooms are divided between the first and second floors. These create groupings for the Mathematics and English departments, as requested. Each floor also has a small

conference room for faculty and honors classes. Underscoring the school's dedication to the arts, an art studio is located at the northern end of each floor. At the center of the building, behind the front doors and across the quad from the old School Building, is an oval entry, called the 'Fauxtunda' in honor of its shallow, but wishful, dome-like ceiling fabricated from a tangle of painted boards. This room leads to stairs up and down, and though it is only slightly wider than a hallway, serves to celebrate the school's next hundred years.

ARCHITECT
Centerbrook Architects and Planners

TYPE OF FACILITY
Preparatory School, 9–12

TYPE OF CONSTRUCTION
New

SITE AREA
1/2 acre on 500 acre campus

BUILDING AREA
20,000 square feet

TOTAL PROJECT COST
$3.4 M

STATUS OF PROJECT
Completed 1995

NUMBER OF STUDENTS
300

STRUCTURAL ENGINEER
Gibble Norden Champion Brown Consulting Engineers

MECHANICAL/ELECTRICAL/CIVIL ENGINEERS
BVH Engineers, Inc.

CONTRACTOR
Inco/Larson Group

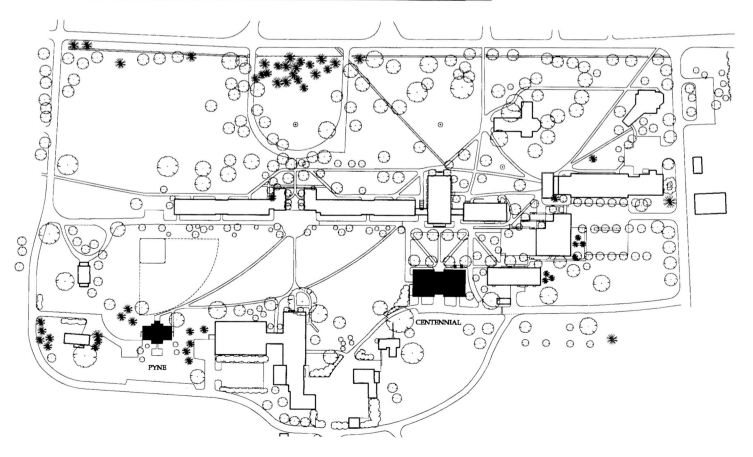

DAKOTA HIGH SCHOOL

MACOMB, MICHIGAN

ARCHITECT'S STATEMENT

The learner is linked to the curricular vision through the physical arrangement of the academic and media center spaces. Science is not a distinct department, but is integrated with social studies, math, and language arts. Many schemes were developed and analyzed by curricular leaders and teaching staff until a final scheme that reflected both an interdisciplinary approach and an ability to return to a departmentalized curriculum was generated.

The design process was extremely interactive and challenging, with many distinct agendas needing to be addressed and satisfied. The final design achieves a complete integration of academic, athletic, fine arts, and community-use agendas while presenting a unified, compact floor plan and a distinctive exterior appearance.

The design has met the primary educational and community needs and is best exemplified by a quote from a leading educator to the principal at the close of a building tour:

'You have no excuse. If your students fail, it is not the fault of the facility. This facility has everything you need for success in the 21st century.'

This high school has received four national educational awards. In addition, The National Science Teachers Association opted to highlight the science classroom-shared science lab arrangement in its recent publication, *NSTA Guide to School Science Facilities*.

ARCHITECT
Fanning/Howey Associates, Inc.

TYPE OF FACILITY
Early Childhood Learning Environment / High School / Innovative Learning Environment

TYPE OF CONSTRUCTION
New

SITE AREA
97 acres

BUILDING AREA
398,000 square feet

TOTAL PROJECT COST
$46,092,300

STATUS OF PROJECT
Completed 1995

NUMBER OF STUDENTS
2,000

STRUCTURAL ENGINEER
Fanning/Howey Associates, Inc.

CONTRACTOR
DeMaria Building Company

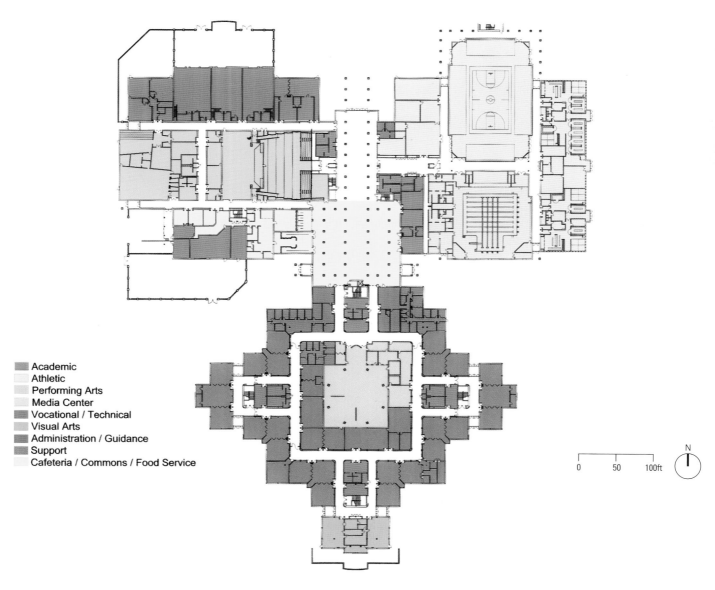

Academic
Athletic
Performing Arts
Media Center
Vocational / Technical
Visual Arts
Administration / Guidance
Support
Cafeteria / Commons / Food Service

0   50   100ft

N

Dakota Ridge High School

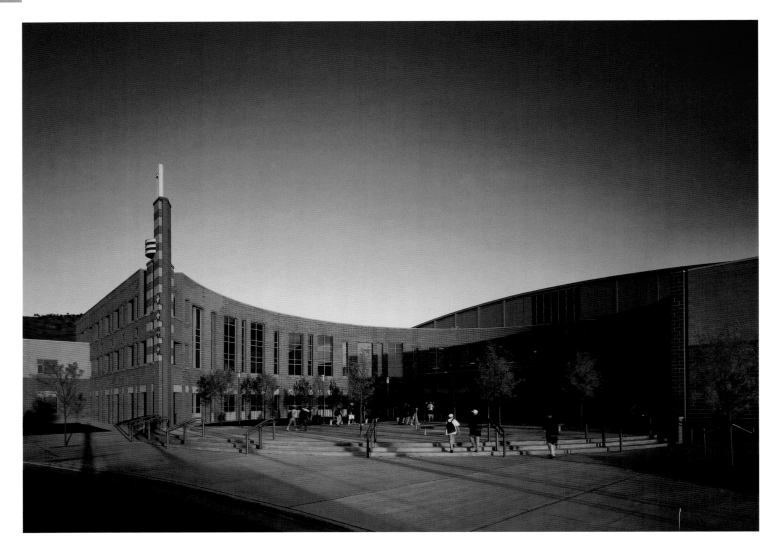

ARCHITECT'S STATEMENT

'To Live. To Love. To Learn. To Leave a Legacy' is the learning signature arrived at by the students of Dakota Ridge High School in a collaborative design process that included parents, teachers, administrators, and the community. The architectural design and the academic program respond to the need to establish a learning environment scaled to engender a community of learners with common interests working together in an interdisciplinary fashion to become lifelong learners.

The campus plan was designed to take advantage of this vast rolling site of high plains grassland, which directly abuts the foothills of the Rockies. Colorado's largest

school district brought a departmentalized education specification to the process and the Design Advisory Group modified that specification to implement an interdisciplinary philosophy. The sprawling suburban community expressed a desire for a high school designed to ultimately serve 2,000 students that was friendly, non-intimidating, and able to serve the needs of individual students.

An on-site committee has established an ongoing assessment process that monitors success, analyzes problems, and develops methods to improve performance.

ARCHITECT
**Klipp Colussy Jenks DuBois
Architects, P.C.**

TYPE OF FACILITY
High School

TYPE OF CONSTRUCTION
New

NUMBER OF STUDENTS
1,250

SITE AREA
42.03 acres

BUILDING AREA
173,120 square feet

TOTAL PROJECT COST
$20,861,360

STATUS OF PROJECT
Completed 1996

STRUCTURAL ENGINEER
JVA, Inc.

MECHANICAL ENGINEER
The Ballard Group

ELECTRICAL ENGINEER
Gambrell Engineering

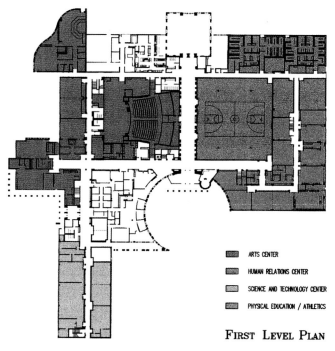

- ARTS CENTER
- HUMAN RELATIONS CENTER
- SCIENCE AND TECHNOLOGY CENTER
- PHYSICAL EDUCATION / ATHLETICS

FIRST LEVEL PLAN

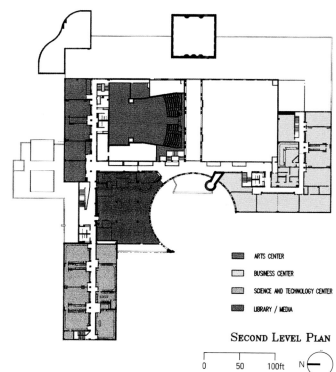

- ARTS CENTER
- BUSINESS CENTER
- SCIENCE AND TECHNOLOGY CENTER
- LIBRARY / MEDIA

SECOND LEVEL PLAN

0   50   100ft   N

EDMONDS-WOODWAY HIGH SCHOOL

EDMONDS, WASHINGTON

ARCHITECT'S STATEMENT

This new high school is the result of an exceptional two-year community design process that included students, parents, teachers, administrators, and community representatives in tandem with district facility managers and architects. This team developed four program themes to direct the design.

Schools must:

- Be adaptable to ongoing educational reform.

- Be flexible to meet multiple learning methodologies yet sustainable to endure for 50 years.

- Integrate technology as an essential learning tool throughout the facility.

- Encourage community partnerships.

The learning clusters adapt to ongoing educational reform by grouping a variety of flexible spaces that can accommodate multiple curriculum scenarios. Each cluster includes classroom, laboratory, teachers prep, conference, and storage spaces grouped around a daylit 'flex area' used for individual research, group projects, and distance learning stations. The great hall, theater, gym, and library are large gathering spaces, designed for both school and community use. Structural, mechanical, and electrical systems are designed to be accessible, expandable, and adaptable.

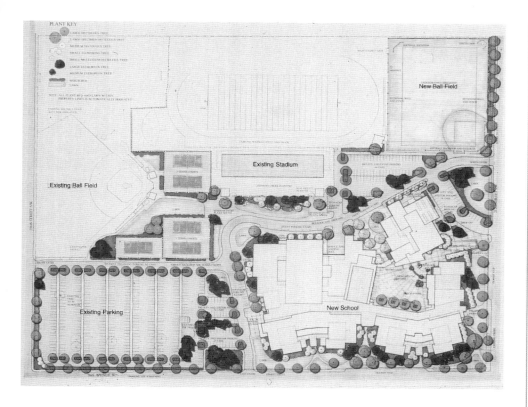

ARCHITECT
Bassetti Architects

TYPE OF FACILITY
High School

TYPE OF CONSTRUCTION
New

SITE AREA
28.5 acres

BUILDING AREA
218,000 square feet

TOTAL PROJECT COST
$43.5 M

STATUS OF PROJECT
Completed 1998

NUMBER OF STUDENTS
1,600

STRUCTURAL ENGINEER
KPFF

MECHANICAL ENGINEER
Wood/Harbinger

ELECTRICAL ENGINEER
Sparling

CONTRACTOR
Lease Crutcher Lewis

GRANDVIEW HIGH SCHOOL

ARCHITECT'S STATEMENT

A deliberate process was initiated to involve a planning/programming committee of 40 people in important decision making throughout programming, master planning, and design phases. Involvement of the committee, facilitated by the architects, took place over a seven-month period. The committee included representation from district and school administrators, education specialists, and a broad spectrum of teachers, students, and parents.

Important initial steps with the committee included a comprehensive research effort focusing on the concepts and issues that shape 'High Schools of the Future.' This study included a detailed analysis of educational programs and resulting organizational concepts.

Following this research, the committee proceeded to define the program for the new school. In addition to space and organizational requirements, this program included 'goals and visions,' statement of educational philosophy, technology goals, objectives for community relationships, security goals, and the district's goals and requirements.

The committee met weekly during the design phase to assure the design accomplished the programmatic needs and to design and develop a school that could be flexible for future changes.

ARCHITECT
H+L/LKA Architects

TYPE OF FACILITY
High School

TYPE OF CONSTRUCTION
New

SITE AREA
79 acres

BUILDING AREA
346,890 square feet

TOTAL PROJECT COST
$40,315,447

STATUS OF PROJECT
Completed 1998

NUMBER OF STUDENTS
2,500

STRUCTURAL ENGINEER
HCDA Engineering

MECHANICAL ENGINEER
MKK Consulting Engineers

ELECTRICAL ENGINEER
Consulting Engineers Inc.

CONTRACTOR
Saunders Construction Inc.

1	Grandview High School	8	Tennis courts
2	Student parking	9	Baseball field
3	Staff/Visitor parking	10	Football/Track
4	Main entrance	11	Softball field
5	Service area	12	Discus/Shotput
6	Dining patio	13	Future addition
7	Soccer field	14	Future play fields

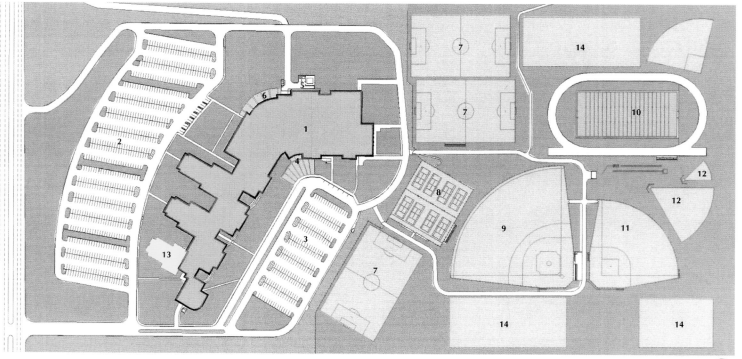

JUAN RODRIGUEZ CABRILLO HIGH SCHOOL

ARCHITECT'S STATEMENT

Program: A large (3,000-student) comprehensive high school for an urban school district in Southern California. The school is built on a 56 acre flat site, in a poor neighborhood on the west end of this coastal city. The district has experienced explosive growth in this area due primarily to immigration.

Solution: The educational program breaks down this large school into smaller components for a better sense of community, more intimacy between students and teachers, and to create responsibility for positive educational outcomes. Grades 9 and 10 are housed in six core clusters of 250 students each, where curriculum centers on core academic skills. Each cluster is composed of six classrooms, two science labs, and a multipurpose/project space. Grades 11 and 12 are centered in three career academies:

arts/communication, science/medical, and business/vocational, where advanced academic classes are integrated with career and vocational training.

Because 30 percent of the teaching stations are required to be in relocatable structures of less than 2,000 square feet each, a portion of the campus was designed to be constructed in the first year as a starter school to house current enrolment. The construction of this school was accomplished in one year from design to occupancy. Construction on the final campus is expected to be completed in August 2002.

Process: The educational planning process was led by the assistant superintendent for secondary education who wanted to create a program model for inner city high schools. The process occurred over a

six-month period with hand-picked, senior district staff. Concurrently, a series of community meetings were held to gather neighborhood input.

ARCHITECT
Thomas Blurock Architects, Inc.

TYPE OF FACILITY
High School

TYPE OF CONSTRUCTION
New

SITE AREA
56 acres

BUILDING AREA
281,844 square feet

TOTAL PROJECT COST
$47,092,830

STATUS OF PROJECT
Estimated completion date
September 2002

NUMBER OF STUDENTS
3,500

STRUCTURAL ENGINEER
Martin, Chow & Nakabara

MECHANICAL ENGINEER
Fundament Associates

ELECTRICAL ENGINEER
Frederick Brown Associates

CONTRACTOR
Hagopian Contractors, Inc.;
Construction Concepts, Inc.;
RC Construction Services, Inc;
Skidmore Contracting CA

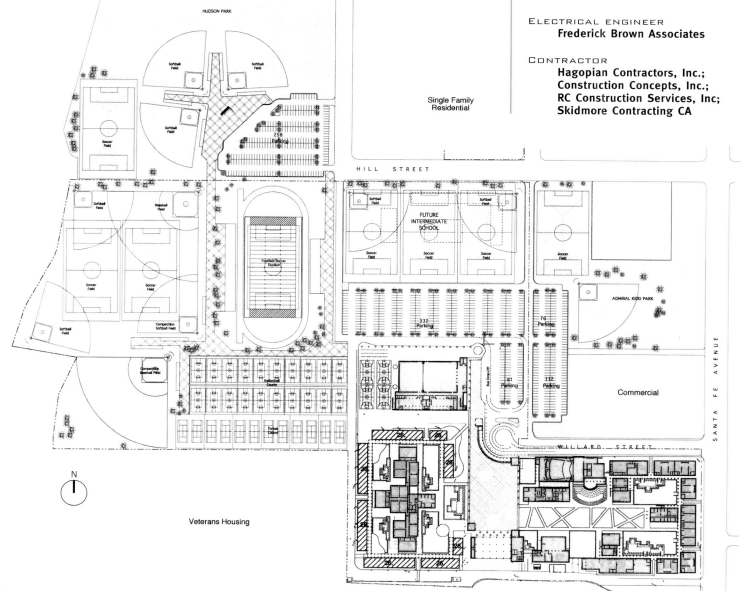

LAKE ORION HIGH SCHOOL

LAKE ORION, MICHIGAN

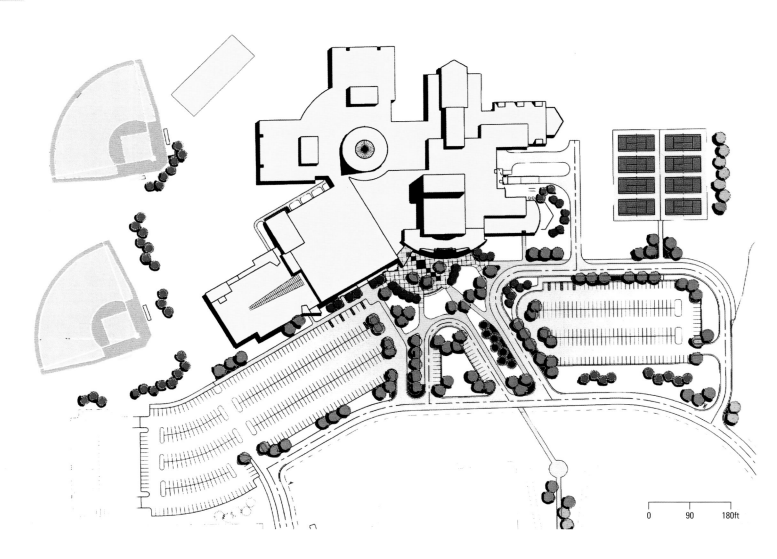

ARCHITECT'S STATEMENT

Including students, staff, administrators, parents, business leaders, citizens, and community leaders in hundreds of hours of interviews, surveys, and meetings did not shorten the nine-month design process for this new high school, but it did assure the district administrators that the design of their new high school would be a unique reflection of the character and image of this rural community! This facility was to be the community's high-tech research and activity center—where the students happen to 'go to school.'

Designers took advantage of the steeply sloped site to provide convenient visitor access to public components of the facility, such as child care, auditorium, gymnasium, and pool, from the upper level parking lots while providing separate student access from a lower floor level carved into the slope. On-site protected wetlands and an

adjacent state park were utilized to provide dramatic vistas and outdoor science learning labs.

This 'student-friendly' facility physically divides the 1,600 students into 400 student 'quads' that include faculty offices, computer labs, group research, and student locker areas. The two-story plan allows each quad to be adjacent to the sky-lit student commons/cafeteria, student services area, and the flexible large group instruction rooms. The media center became part of a tech center that includes distance learning, science, journalism, art, radio/TV, and tech-ed studios.

The resulting community-friendly facility reflects a progressive high-tech character and contemporary image while also preserving the accountability and individuality of each learner!

ARCHITECT
URS Corporation

TYPE OF FACILITY
High School

TYPE OF CONSTRUCTION
New

SITE AREA
80 acres

BUILDING AREA
377,756 square feet

TOTAL PROJECT COST
$56,049,680

STATUS OF PROJECT
Completed August 1998

NUMBER OF STUDENTS
1,600

STRUCTURAL/MECHANICAL/
ELECTRICAL ENGINEER
URS Corporation

CONTRACTOR
Barton Malow Company

LICK-WILMERDING LIBRARY/ARTS & HUMANITIES BUILDING

SAN FRANCISCO, CALIFORNIA

ARCHITECT'S STATEMENT

Founded in 1895 as a technical arts school, its educational philosophy combines rigorous college preparation with offerings in the technical, performing, and visual arts. In 1989 we were selected to develop a master plan to address the school's long-term physical needs. The result of the process is a trusting and creative collaboration between architect and client.

The new library/arts and humanities building is in every way a physical manifestation of the school's mission, purpose, and curriculum. Its educational program is based on the dictum, 'Head, Heart, Hands' (Head: The education of the mind. Heart: The nurturing of a social conscience. Hands: The training of applied

skills). For example, our design specified the use of exposed structure and a skin composed of assembled industrial products, as a continued reflection of the hands-on teaching at the center of the school's philosophy. To accommodate the three-tiered structure of the academic program, we created a variety of settings from an 8,000 square foot open-plan library to small group study/conference spaces in which the rich and diverse education offered by the school can generously take place. The design recognizes the validity of departmental identities while making numerous explicit and implicit connections among disciplines.

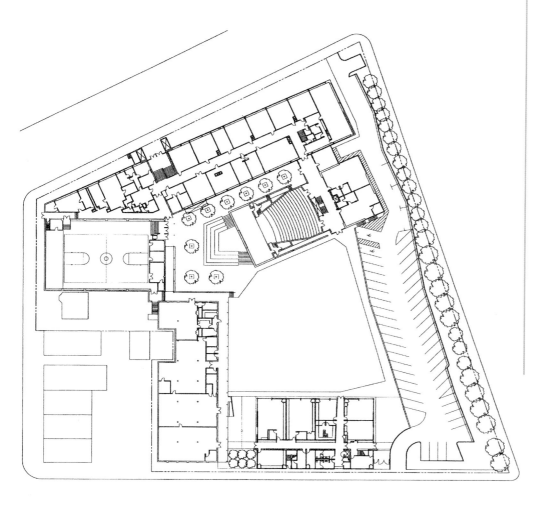

ARCHITECT
SMWM

TYPE OF FACILITY
High School Library and Academic Buildings

TYPE OF CONSTRUCTION
New

SITE AREA
3.1 acres

BUILDING AREA
17,600 square feet

TOTAL PROJECT COST
$3.5 M

STATUS OF PROJECT
Completed 1997

NUMBER OF STUDENTS
399

STRUCTURAL ENGINEER
Tipping Mar & Associates

MECHANICAL ENGINEER
JYA Consulting Engineers

ELECTRICAL ENGINEER
O'Mahony & Myer

CONTRACTOR
Plant Construction Company

MANHATTAN VILLAGE ACADEMY HIGH SCHOOL

ARCHITECT'S STATEMENT

New York City Board of Education's Manhattan Village Academy High School (MVA)—a small school, called an 'alternative' school, was designed for 400 students. The school's sponsor, the Center for Collaborative Education, was founded by MacArthur Foundation Award grantee Deborah Meiers. Mary Butz, the school's principal, and Ms Meiers rejected the Board of Education's proposed 'factory model'—a standard classroom plan off of a winding corridor. Based on her experience, Ms Meier believes that corridors are a place of potential violence. Ms Meiers and Ms Butz wanted clustered, flexible space with minimum corridor connections to fit their concept of personalized education

and project teaching. To create a customized program to fit their pedagogy, Ms Meier and the architect together visited a number of well-designed schools with innovative ideas. However, none fit their pedagogy. The architect then developed the 'locus' plan—a cluster of classrooms for each grade (100 students) around an interior 'quad' space, where teachers have the choice of a variety of spaces and space sizes to fit their personalized approach to the student needs.

Approximately 70 percent of MVA's students come from urban minority families. The architect and the client designed the school's environment to be student friendly—respectful, calming, and

serene. The intent of the quality of the design was to dignify the idea of education and its importance; and support the administration, teaching, and learning process. That every senior of the first graduating class went to college is testimony to the success of the educators and the design. The school is located in two floors of two existing office towers. It has a separate street level entrance at 43 West 22nd Street. The interior build-out was designed and constructed within 12 months, on schedule and on budget.

1 Classroom
2 Science/Math classroom
3 Read/Study area
4 Art room
5 Bicycle shop
6 Cafeteria
7 Warming pantry
8 Kitchen storage
9 Culinary arts classroom
10 Kitchen staff / Changing room
11 Social worker's office
12 Student advisor's office
13 Principal's office
14 Assistant principal's office
15 Secretary
16 Conference room
17 General office
18 Staff room
19 Attendance office
20 Equipment room
21 Gallery

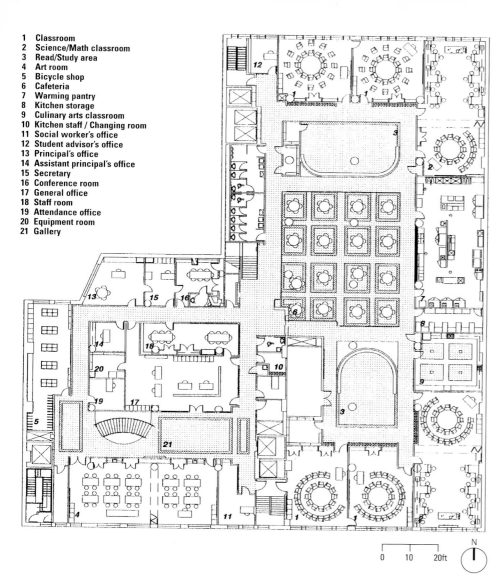

ARCHITECT
Beverly Willis Architects

TYPE OF FACILITY
High School / Alternative School

TYPE OF CONSTRUCTION
Renovation

BUILDING AREA
60,000 square feet

TOTAL PROJECT COST
$6 M

STATUS OF PROJECT
Completed 1995

NUMBER OF STUDENTS
350

STRUCTURAL ENGINEER
Thornton-Tomasetti Engineers

MECHANICAL/ELECTRICAL
ENGINEER
Robert Derector & Associates

CONTRACTOR
Lehr Constructions

0   10   20ft

N

NEW MAGNET PROGRAM—CENTER FOR PRE-LAW & LEGAL STUDIES

WEST PALM BEACH, FLORIDA

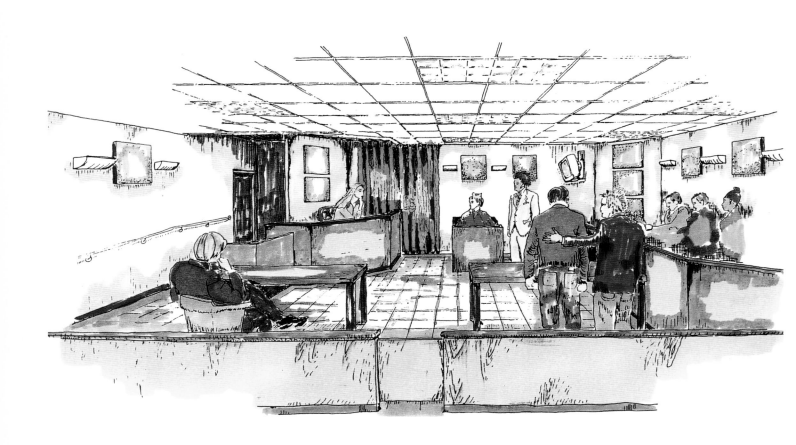

ARCHITECT'S STATEMENT

The school district wanted to start a new magnet program for legal studies in order to achieve a more desirable racial mix at an urban school. The proposed school had approximately 2,800 square feet of administrative space, that could be converted for the program. The principal and the school board agreed to give up the administrative space, if the designated space could be renovated for the new magnet program for legal studies.

Under a design/build contract, the architect and general contractor met with school district architects, the magnet program coordinator, the assistant principal, and teachers in the program. The primary goal of the renovation was to ensure 'that the finished space looked and felt exactly like

a courtroom.' Other needs included a law library, jury room, judge's office, and general classroom. Preliminary budgets and plans were developed from these meetings. Perspective sketches were developed to convey the 'look and feel' of the space, and to verify the program goal would be met.

The school district solicited donations of courtroom furniture from the local court system, in order to save on project costs. Thus the design had to accommodate unspecified furniture, which could change as the design developed. The approximate design time was three months and the approximate construction time was six months.

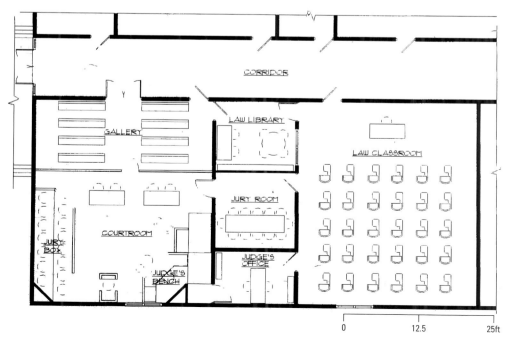

ARCHITECT
Jon Bloss Blehar, AIA, PA.,
Architect

TYPE OF FACILITY
High School

TYPE OF CONSTRUCTION
Renovation

BUILDING AREA
2,812 square feet

TOTAL PROJECT COST
$180,000

STATUS OF PROJECT
Completed 1998

NUMBER OF STUDENTS
200

MECHANICAL ENGINEER
RGD & Associates Inc.

ELECTRICAL ENGINEER
Gillespie & Associates, Inc.

CONTRACTOR
MCC Construction Corp.

NEW SOUTHWEST HIGH SCHOOL

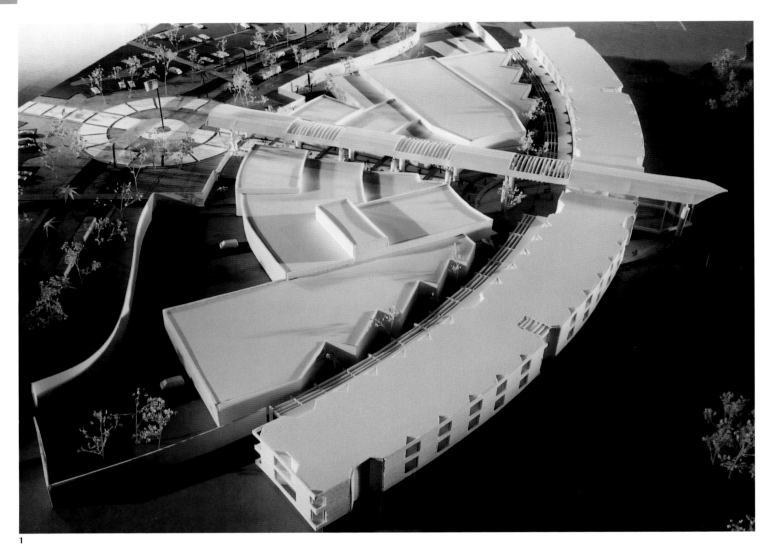

1

ARCHITECT'S STATEMENT

Organized around the central common area, the 'Atrio,' the school shares its resources openly with the community it serves. Traditionally, in historic southwest architecture, the Atrio was the central gathering place in front of the town church. It was used for instruction, music, dance, and processions and was the focus of community life. The characteristics of the Atrio are very appropriate to a high school environment that fosters a strong and lasting sense of community—thus, this design organizes the school around this active space.

The Atrio is approached through a tall, arcaded gateway that originates at the south main entry. This galleria forms a strong linear vista to the Atrio terminating at the media center, which symbolically represents the heart of the learning environment. From the Atrio, access to

the media center, theater, and gymnasium is clear and direct. Flanking the Atrio to the east and west are covered pedestrian ramadas linking all parts of the school back to the main gathering area. This outdoor space is shaded, allowing performances, festivals, and school special events to occur in an appropriate setting.

Building forms were derived to respond to site influences and to create flexible and expandable learning environments. Classrooms are flexible in design to allow teaming, cooperative learning, and interdisciplinary teaching to occur. All class areas include carefully articulated windows to take full advantage of the setting. The gentle east-west curve of the circulation spine and ramada allows breezes to be captured for natural cooling and provides 'friendly' visual supervision to all parts of the academic core. The media center, at

the heart of this core, allows easy access for students and community to enjoy the resources contained within. Additionally, future expansion of this core can be accommodated in four locations adding to the flexibility.

ARCHITECT
**TMP Associates, Inc.;
The IEF Group**

TYPE OF FACILITY
High School

TYPE OF CONSTRUCTION
New

SITE AREA
60 acres

BUILDING AREA
230,000 square feet

STATUS OF PROJECT
Not built

NUMBER OF STUDENTS
2000

STRUCTURAL ENGINEER
Holben, Martin & Meza

MECHANICAL ENGINEER
Adams & Associates, Inc.

ELECTRICAL ENGINEER
Morand Engineering, Inc.

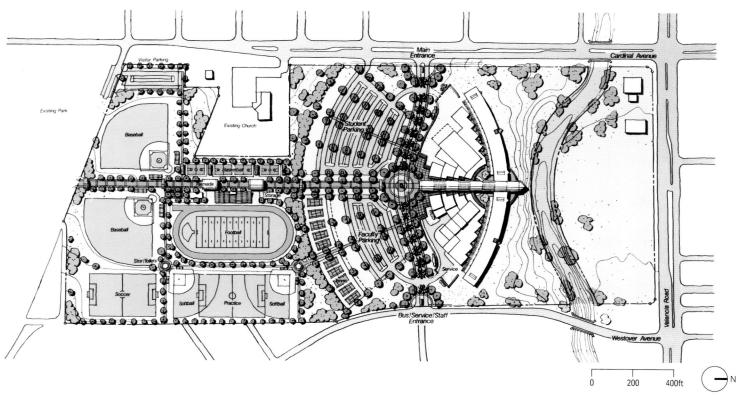

New Technology High School

Architect's statement

Working in cooperation with high-tech industry and community agencies, the school district embarked on a new innovative high school program to prepare students to enter a high technology career or college. The school's mission is to build a bridge between education and business and create a curriculum that prepares students to succeed and compete in an advanced technology-based society.

In partnership with technology leaders such as Silicon Graphics and Hewlett-Packard, the architects and district created a high school which serves as a nationally recognized model for the use of technology in education. Emphasizing an environment modeled after the business workplace, each student has a custom workstation provided with his/her own high performance networked computer.

National recognition: since its completion, the New Technology High School is a US Department of Education Demonstration Site, a California Department of Education Tech Prep Development Site, was the site for congressional hearings on education reform, was the model for the California Digital High School legislation, and has been featured nationally on CNN, NBC, and Bay Area stations.

Designed after business workplace: using models from high-tech industry such as Hewlett Packard and Silicon Graphics.

Celebration of technology: the exposed data network and distribution equipment celebrate the school's technological infrastructure rather than hiding it in walls.

Open space design: the building's open plan allowed the architects to provide large glass walls, promoting a sense of community and views while maintaining acoustical privacy.

ARCHITECT
Quattrocchi Kwok Architects

TYPE OF FACILITY
High School / Innovative Learning Environment

TYPE OF CONSTRUCTION
Renovation

BUILDING AREA
24,997 square feet

TOTAL PROJECT COST
$810,000

STATUS OF PROJECT
Completed September 1996

NUMBER OF STUDENTS
350

STRUCTURAL ENGINEER
Zucco Fagent Associates

MECHANICAL ENGINEER
Horn Engineers

ELECTRICAL ENGINEER
Myers Engineering Group

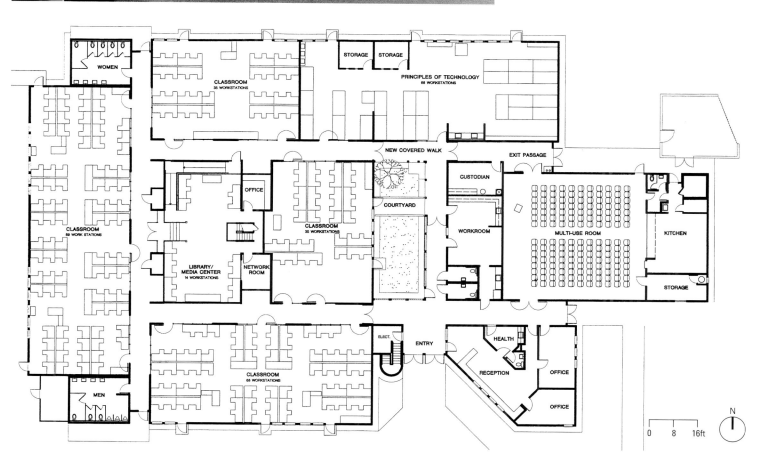

OXFORD HILLS COMPREHENSIVE HIGH SCHOOL

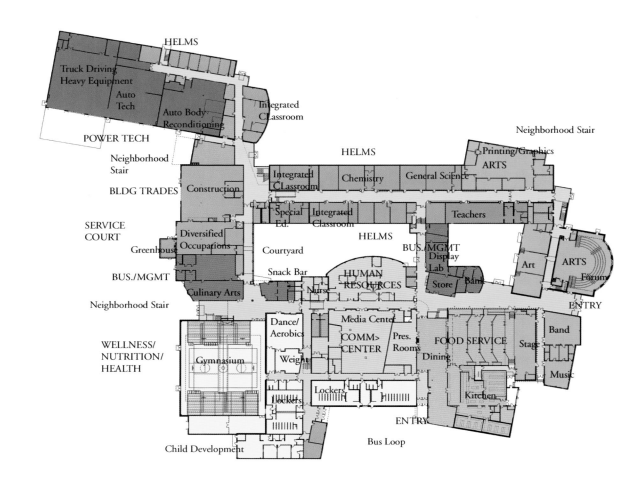

ARCHITECT'S STATEMENT

This project integrates a regional academic high school and a technical high school in one building with separate, cooperative administrations and faculty. The educational vision is a 'seamless' school integrating both paths and offering all students hands-on learning. Additions surround the original building, which was completely reorganized and renovated.

Community meetings conceived 10 core elements, including: flexible building and educational structures, small-scale learning environments, and integration of school and community. A Concept Team refined organizational concepts:

- Six clusters, each with specific learning focus. Students choose their own clusters.
- Three neighborhoods, each with a pair of clusters, surround faculty areas, computers, stairs, and toilets.

- History, English, language, math, and science (HELMS) in all clusters.
- Central human resources area combining administration, guidance, adult education, athletics, and nurse.
- Public mall linking community use elements.
- Integrated classrooms, designed for two teachers, with conference rooms and wet areas.

The community has gained:

- a meeting/recreational center
- a branch of the state university and technical colleges
- a center for adult education
- a regional business venue.

ARCHITECT
PDT Architects

TYPE OF FACILITY
High School

TYPE OF CONSTRUCTION
Addition/Renovation

SITE AREA
25 + 25 acres

BUILDING AREA
277,046 square feet

TOTAL PROJECT COST
$28,964,200

STATUS OF PROJECT
Completed 1998

NUMBER OF STUDENTS
1,240

STRUCTURAL/MECHANICAL/
ELECTRICAL ENGINEER
Allied Engineering Inc.

CIVIL ENGINEER
DeLuca Hoffman Associates, Inc.

CONTRACTOR
Granger Northern, Inc.

PHELPS SCIENCE CENTER, PHILLIPS EXETER ACADEMY

EXETER, NEW HAMPSHIRE

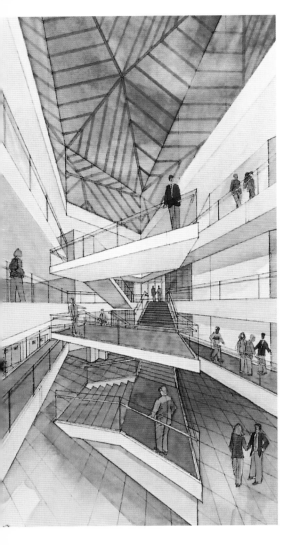

ARCHITECT'S STATEMENT

This well-known private preparatory school has for many years used a teaching method focused on the 'Harkness Table,' a 7 x 11 foot oval table that accommodates 12 students and a teacher who present and discuss their work in a group participation format. This method has not previously been used for science.

The program for this new science building is to adapt the Harkness method of teaching to the science curriculum. The architects were asked to completely rethink typical educational laboratory design to accommodate this pedagogical approach.

To accomplish the institution's desire to include the entire academic community in the design process, the architects used a series of design workshops which included faculty, students, administration, trustees, local residents, and village officials. The product of these workshops is a design that includes the best ideas of more than 70 interested participants representing a broad spectrum of the institution and the community.

In addition to the programmatic needs, the building had to fit comfortably in a handsome New England campus that has evolved over more than 200 years. To test the workability and verify this unique design, a prototype classroom was built in the existing science building and tested by faculty and students for more than a year. During that time, refinements and modifications were made to the classroom design. The prototype classroom included testing of a variety of furniture, equipment, laboratory benches, and audio-visual technology for accessing information and distance learning.

ARCHITECT
Centerbrook Architects and Planners

TYPE OF FACILITY
Preparatory School

TYPE OF CONSTRUCTION
New

NUMBER OF STUDENTS
1,000

SITE AREA
5 acres

BUILDING AREA
73,000 square feet

TOTAL PROJECT COST
$26.9 M

STATUS OF PROJECT
Estimated completion date August 2001

LABORATORY/CLASSROOM PLANNERS
Harley Ellis

STRUCTURAL/GEOTECHNICAL ENGINEERS
Gibble Norden Champion Consulting Engineers

MECHANICAL/ELECTRICAL
Bard Rao + Athanas Consulting Engineers

CIVIL ENGINEERS
Rist-Frost Shurnway Engineering, P.C.

LANDSCAPE ARCHITECT
Michael Van Valkenburgh Associates, Inc.

CONTRACTOR
Pizzagalli Construction Company

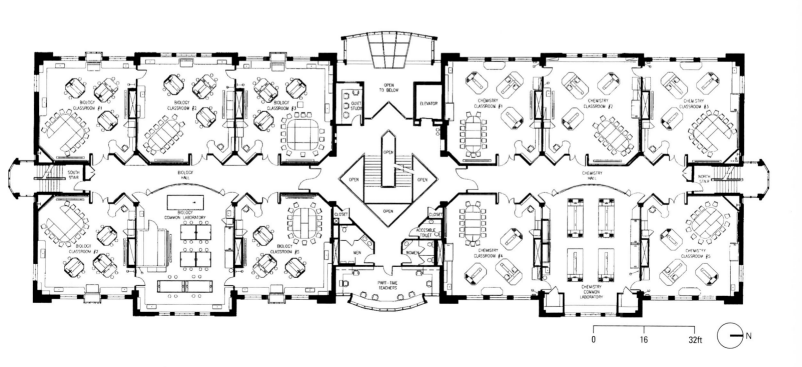

0   16   32ft   N

STAR VALLEY HIGH SCHOOL

AFTON, WYOMING

ARCHITECT'S STATEMENT

The new Star Valley High School is the first new high school in this district in over 60 years; and will be the community center for the entire county. It is designed for 800 students (growth is planned to accommodate 1,200 students) with the latest state-of-the-art technological advances. It is also used year-round for numerous adult education classes including business skills courses and is the primary community center for a variety of uses and activities.

The education specifications/facility program was completed by the architect prior to commencing the design. The design solution responded to the unusual scheduling needs of the facility and resolved many of the owner's curriculum problems. The new school is designed to facilitate curriculum changes while responding to specific programmatic goals.

ARCHITECT
Valentiner Crane Brunjes Onyon Architects

TYPE OF FACILITY
High School / Innovative Learning Environment / Other or Multipurpose

TYPE OF CONSTRUCTION
New

NUMBER OF STUDENTS
1,200

BUILDING AREA
220,000 square feet

TOTAL PROJECT COST
$26.2 M

STATUS OF PROJECT
Completed August 1998

STRUCTURAL ENGINEER
Bsumek Mu and Associates

MECHANICAL ENGINEER
Bennion and Associates Engineers

ELECTRICAL ENGINEER
BNA Consulting Engineers II

CONTRACTOR
Hogan & Associates

WAVERLY HIGH SCHOOL

WAVERLY, NEBRASKA

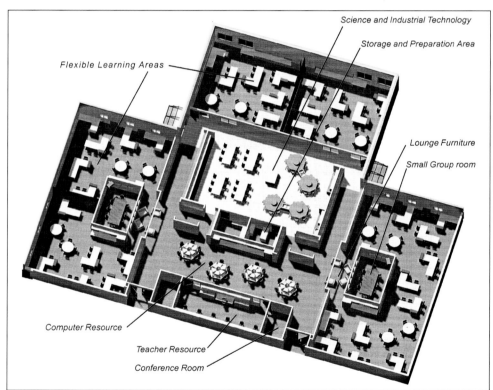

Science and Industrial Technology

Storage and Preparation Area

Flexible Learning Areas

Lounge Furniture

Small Group room

Computer Resource

Teacher Resource

Conference Room

ARCHITECT'S STATEMENT

The design was to create a flexible learning environment for 700 9th through 12th grade students to encourage the following educational approaches: block scheduling, cross disciplinary team teaching, thematic curricula, and project-based learning. Community use of the facility required multiple options for securing portions of the facility.

The planning and design process incorporated extensive involvement with a citizens' committee. After the architect completed a facility study with staff input the citizens' committee then prioritized needs in subcommittees. Notes on large paper were taped to the walls and used to present to the whole committee.

After the prioritized needs were presented, the citizen's committee was asked to complete the following: 'What if we …?'

This activity provided the bridge between needs and solutions. The result remained the property of the committee, not the designer.

The consensus building process moved toward an agreement on a new high school and site. The architects toured other schools with key staff and administrators and then jointly developed requirements for a flexible cross-disciplinary learning house and all other specialized learning areas.

ARCHITECT
The Architectural Partnership, P.C.

TYPE OF FACILITY
High School

TYPE OF CONSTRUCTION
New

SITE AREA
78 acres

BUILDING AREA
125,000 square feet

TOTAL PROJECT COST
$11,175,642

STATUS OF PROJECT
Completed 1998

NUMBER OF STUDENTS
700

STRUCTURAL ENGINEER
The Architectural Partnership, P.C.

MECHANICAL/ELECTRICAL
ENGINEER
Fred Thompson & Associates

CONTRACTOR
General/Sampson Construction Co.

1	Flexible Learning Areas	10	Distance Learning	20	Machines
2	Science & Industrial	11	Special Education	21	Woods
	Technology	12	Media Center	22	Weight Room
3	Computer Resource	13	Business	23	Kitchen
4	Small Group	14	Family & Consumer Service	24	Cafeteria/Commons
5	Teacher Resource	15	Journalism & Business	25	Theater
6	Conference Room	16	Art	26	Women's Locker
7	Storage & Preparation	17	Chior/Drama	27	Men's Locker
8	Administration	18	Band	28	Gymnasium
9	Counseling	19	Welding/Auto		

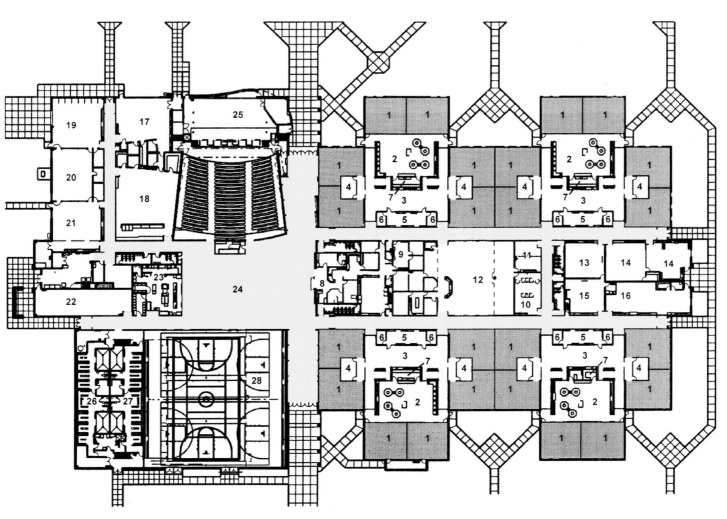

ALPHA HIGH SCHOOL

HONOR

ARCHITECT'S STATEMENT

This alternative high school may very well be an example of the adage 'great things come in small packages' although in this case it might be 'great things happen in small packages.' In a modest 16,000 square feet, the facility provides all the academic opportunities of a traditional high school; in addition, it is home to businesses that take advantage of inexpensive space in exchange for training students. The building also accommodates demonstration areas for potential job sites outside the school; evening college courses; community meeting space; and the headquarters for a student-run clearinghouse coordinating student volunteers for community projects.

Getting everything into the school required multiple solutions. First, the physical size of the rooms was made adjustable through the combined use of operable partitions and a brand new system of moving walls developed by the architect. Second, storage cabinets, teacher stations, student project lockers, tables, computer carts, and desks were all designed to be mobile. Finally, data locations, lighting, mechanical systems, and finishes were all designed to contribute to the flexibility of the building.

The result is a building that does not merely accommodate a wide range of functions, but can be modified to enhance the changing activities of the school.

N.E. 8TH STREET

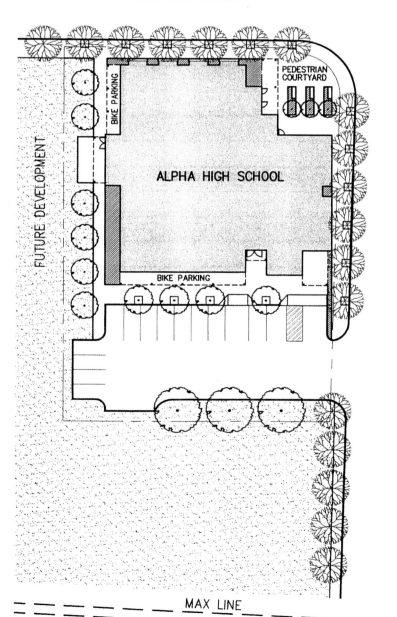

ARCHITECT
Dull Olson Weekes Architects

TYPE OF FACILITY
Alternative High School

TYPE OF CONSTRUCTION
New

SITE AREA
1.5 acres

BUILDING AREA
16,000 square feet

TOTAL PROJECT COST
$3,012,000

STATUS OF PROJECT
Completed February 1999

NUMBER OF STUDENTS
184

STRUCTURAL ENGINEER
Kpff Consulting Engineers

MECHANICAL ENGINEER
Accipio Inc. Consulting Engineers

ELECTRICAL ENGINEER
Cundiff Engineering

CONTRACTOR
Devcon Construction Company

SCHOOL FOR THE PHYSICAL CITY

ARCHITECT'S STATEMENT

The School for the Physical City, one of the 'small schools' inaugurated by the New York City Board of Education in 1993–94, moved to these new quarters at the beginning of the fall 1995 semester. Occupying 55,000 square feet of space on floors 1–5 of a Manhattan office building, the school accommodates a maximum of 500 students at the intermediate and high school levels. An underlying purpose of the school is to broaden students' education by introducing them to the urban infrastructure, using the city's resources as a learning laboratory.

In keeping with this theme, the school has been designed as a means by which students can learn about the built environment through observing the elements that make up the building. Structural columns on every floor are painted a vivid green. Overhead water

pipes are painted blue; air-conditioning ducts are in a variety of colors. At the same juncture on every floor there is a small viewing panel (painted green) that lets one see into the room containing the heating, ventilation and air-conditioning equipment for that floor.

Other distinctive design elements include color-coding of public spaces and classrooms according to use; floor and wall markings that orient students to compass directions and to the height of each floor above street level; a floor plan on every floor; and a lobby desk constructed of steel beams in homage to Peter Cooper, founder of The Cooper Union (a co-sponsor of the school), who pioneered steel-frame construction—a basic component of the 20th-century building's infrastructure.

Special attention was paid to making provision for the school to be fully computerized. Extra space was set aside for the addition of telecommunications and power-wiring in the future.

ARCHITECT
**Rothzeid Kaiserman
Thomson & Bee**

TYPE OF FACILITY
**Middle/Junior High School / High
School / Alternative School**

TYPE OF CONSTRUCTION
Renovation

BUILDING AREA
55,000 square feet

TOTAL PROJECT COST
$5.7 M

STATUS OF PROJECT
Completed 1995

NUMBER OF STUDENTS
400–500

STRUCTURAL ENGINEER
**Selnick/Harwood Consulting
Engineers**

MECHANICAL/ELECTRICAL
ENGINEER
**George Langer Associates
Consulting Engineers**

CONTRACTOR
M.D. Carlisle Construction Group

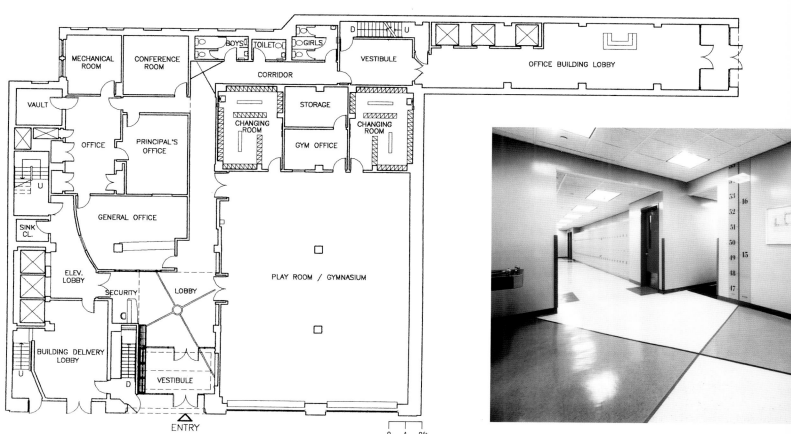

EDUCATIONAL FACILITIES

INNOVATIVE LEARNING ENVIRONMENTS

ADAM JOSEPH LEWIS CENTER FOR ENVIRONMENTAL STUDIES

OBERLIN, OHIO

ARCHITECT'S STATEMENT

This project represents the vision of an enlightened client and educator who believes in 'architecture as pedagogy.' The goal the client gave the design team was to create a building that embodies a curriculum of mindfulness and ecological competence, in addition to providing offices, classrooms, and gathering spaces.

The design team met this challenge by creating a building that is an explicit model of sustainability. The project incorporates numerous advanced features to optimize environmental impact, including photovoltics, fuel cells, geothermal wells, passive solar design, a created wetland and pond to handle storm water, and a 'Living

Machine' to treat and recycle waste water using natural processes. The result is a building designed to become a net energy exporter, and to emit nothing dangerous.

While the sustainability of the project is central to its design, the building also meets high aesthetic standards. It fits harmoniously into the campus, and provides comfortable and uplifting spaces for a variety of activities.

ARCHITECT
William McDonough + Partners

TYPE OF FACILITY
Innovative Learning Environment

TYPE OF CONSTRUCTION
New

SITE AREA
Approx. 1.5 acres

BUILDING AREA
13,600 square feet

TOTAL PROJECT COST
$6,110,000

STATUS OF PROJECT
Completed 2000

NUMBER OF STUDENTS
2,905

STRUCTURAL/MECHANICAL/
ELECTRICAL ENGINEER
Lev Zetlin Associates

CONTRACTOR
Mosser Construction, Inc.

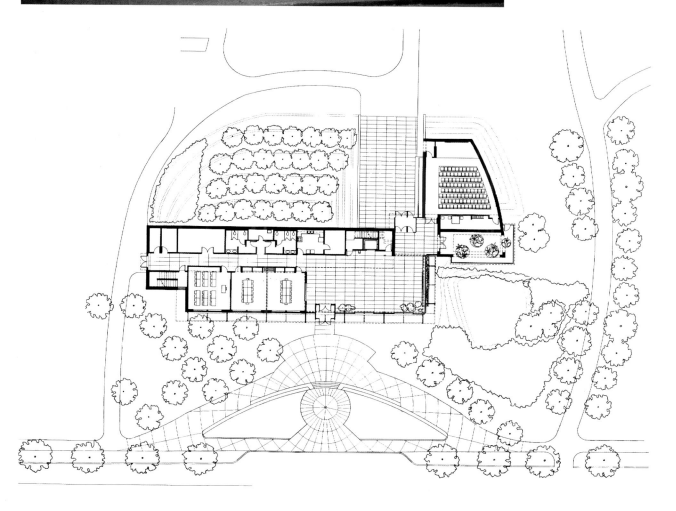

EarthWorks

ARCHITECT'S STATEMENT

The Learning Exchange is a Kansas City-based not-for-profit educational consulting agency specializing in unique learning environments. Based on the agency's past success, the idea emerged to create a hands-on learning environment that would teach children how the 'earth works.' The program attracted funding from several prominent local corporations, including H&R Block and Hallmark.

A unique and dramatic site immediately suggested itself for such a project: Kansas City's vast Hunt Midwest 'Subtropolis,' a 50 million square foot subterranean complex created by limestone mining operations in the early 1900s. Situating EarthWorks in such a setting allowed the facility to take advantage of the natural insulation properties of a cave. It also offered students an exciting and memorable environment outside the classroom.

An irregularly shaped space was created to host activities related to the five different ecosystems: soil, prairie, pond, cave, and forest. Each ecosystem is connected to the next by a sinuous wooden walkway and dioramas for each ecosystem lead directly to shelters for pedagogical experiments.

Today EarthWorks hosts 10,000 third- and fourth-graders annually. Students participate in a six-week pre-visit curriculum in which they prepare for their excursion. At EarthWorks they function as scientists: gathering data, testing hypotheses, and documenting their findings. As they work together they gain insights into what makes a healthy and sustainable environment possible.

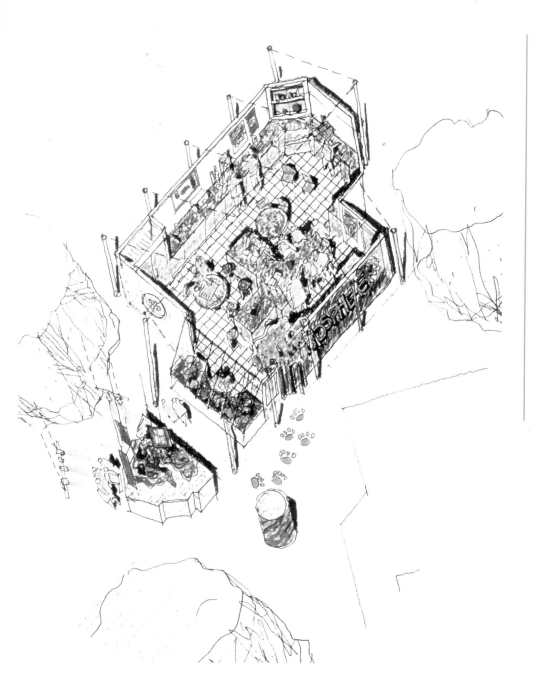

ARCHITECT
BNIM Architects

TYPE OF FACILITY
Innovative Learning Environment

TYPE OF CONSTRUCTION
New

SITE AREA
1.2 acres

BUILDING AREA
42,000 square feet

TOTAL PROJECT COST
$1.1 M

STATUS OF PROJECT
Completed April 1996

STRUCTURAL ENGINEER
Structural Engineering Associates

MECHANICAL ENGINEER
Gibbens Drake Scott Engineering Inc.

CONTRACTOR
J. E. Dunn Construction Company

Grainger Center for Imagination and Inquiry

AURORA, ILLINOIS

1

ARCHITECT'S STATEMENT

The team designed a laboratory within an existing school of advanced mathematics and science. One of the public/private research organizations supporting the school's programs funded the Center for Imagination and Inquiry (CII). This is not the typical high school science lab. At CII, students 'lease' space while pursuing independent studies under corporate mentorship. Students must submit proposals defining their research—any imaginable experiment within the realms of science and technology. Understanding the needs for an infinitely flexible laboratory, the architects utilized a detailed Web questionnaire to query students and teachers about their desired facility.

Proposed fields for inclusion ranged from 'traditional' sciences (geology, genetics, chaos theory) to technological invention (robotics, microchip fabrication) to revolutionary explorations ('the lab as theatre'). The team diagrammed layers of flexibility and analyzed options. The final design offers layers of flexibility involving elements such as flexible data/power hook-ups; mobile work stations/mini-labs to be grouped for collaborative work or positioned independently; fixed and flexible 'think tanks;' and even experiments using the lab, itself, as theater.

Students are limited only by their imaginations.

ARCHITECT
OWP&P, Chicago, Illinois

TYPE OF FACILITY
**High School / Innovative
Learning Environment**

TYPE OF CONSTRUCTION
Renovation

BUILDING AREA
2,840 square feet

TOTAL PROJECT COST
$500,000

STATUS OF PROJECT
Completed August 1999

NUMBER OF STUDENTS
40 (lab); 660 (academy)

STRUCTURAL/MECHANICAL/
ELECTRICAL ENGINEER
OWP&P

CONTRACTOR
Multitech LLC

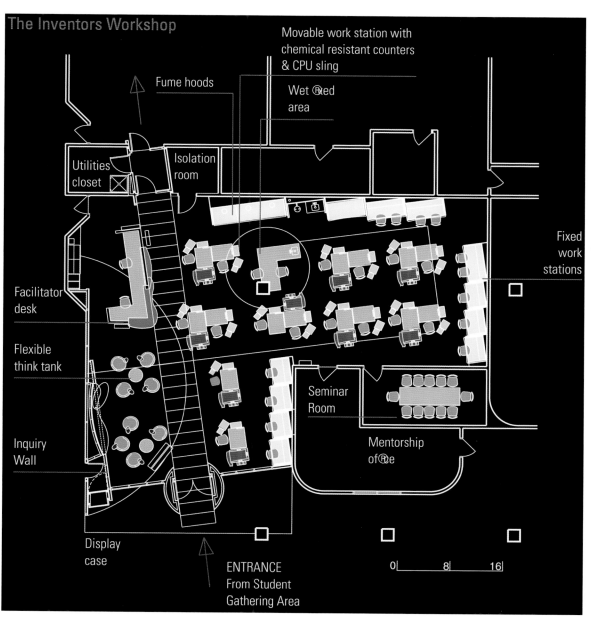

The Inventors Workshop

Movable work station with chemical resistant counters & CPU sling

Fume hoods

Wet fixed area

Utilities closet

Isolation room

Facilitator desk

Fixed work stations

Flexible think tank

Seminar Room

Inquiry Wall

Mentorship office

Display case

ENTRANCE
From Student
Gathering Area

0   8   16

KidPower/New York Hall of Science Playground

Citation

Architect's statement

The 30,000 square foot teaching park, KidPower, has been created to augment the interior exhibits of the New York Hall of Science museum, encouraging visitors to learn principles of physics through their interaction with large-scale, outdoor exhibits. A linear bridge-like structure that runs the length of the teaching park, provides a visual connection from the museum's new front entrance to the primary pedestrian path in Flushing Meadow Park. It also provides two important viewing vantage points, animating the museum building's visual appeal in dramatic new ways. This is seen as a renewal of the World's Fair spirit that still pervades the site after 30+ years. The dramatic sculptural quality of the teaching park's built structure functions as an invitation to the community to discover the museum, and in turn as an invitation for those in the museum to explore the teaching park.

The large scale elements of the teaching park structure are designed to act as exhibits themselves, displaying mechanical means of attachment like a giant erector set. A series of steel pylons carry a continuous metal tube and a suspended walkway alongside the Hall of Science terrace. The suspended walkway is a staging platform for activities that use gravity or need height in dealing with motion and balance. The structure becomes an organizing element for the exhibits, with the regular rhythm of the pylons providing a subtle sense of order within the exuberance of the shapes and colours that comprise the physical activities. Likewise, the alternating stripes of the resilient surfacing speak of order amidst the fun. A boardwalk, which makes an undulating edge along the outside of the park, holds a series of water exhibits and mirrors the shape of the Hall of Science building. The boardwalk acts as an engaging transition from the teaching park

to the area that borders the Flushing Meadows Park. Here, somewhat away from the active exhibits, adults can supervise smaller children at play.

School groups take great advantage of collaborative play activities that the teaching park makes possible. To accommodate these groups, an outdoor eating area, directly accessible from the Hall of Science lunchroom, is cut into the earth with a robustly-scaled sheet piling retaining wall. While sitting below the retaining wall in the eating area, or even on the ramp that rises alongside it, one can sense the force of the earth on which the park sits.

The project team worked together closely to achieve a synthesis of the architectural, structural, landscape, and exhibit aspects of the park, with all parts contributing to the educational goal of translating sophisticated scientific ideas into full body play.

ARCHITECT
BKS/K Architects

TYPE OF FACILITY
Innovative Learning Environment

TYPE OF CONSTRUCTION
New

NUMBER OF STUDENTS
250

SITE AREA
30,000 square feet

TOTAL PROJECT COST
$3.3 M

STATUS OF PROJECT
Completed 1997

LANDSCAPE ARCHITECT
Lee Weintraub, Landscape Architecture

EXHIBIT PLANNING CONSULTANT
Jane Clark, Chermayeff Associates

EXHIBIT DESIGN
Chermayeff and Geismar

STRUCTURAL ENGINEER
Weidlinger Associates

MECHANICAL/ELECTRICAL ENGINEER
Lilker Associates

CONTRACTOR
Stonewall Contracting

RUSK CHILDREN'S PLAYGARDEN FOR INTERACTIVE THERAPEUTIC PLAY

ARCHITECT'S STATEMENT

The team of therapeutic professionals at the Rusk Institute of Rehabilitation Medicine, NYU Medical Center, wanted to challenge their young patients within a supportive and nature-oriented outdoor environment. The landscape architect, horticultural, physical, occupational, recreational, and music therapists, pre-school teachers, and other medical personnel, collaborated extensively during the design process in order to achieve this goal.

We transformed a tiny, flat, urban lot into an exciting and educational multi-level environment for physically disabled children. Custom-built play equipment is fully integrated with natural processes and features—promoting curiosity, creativity, and independence. The friendly scale of undulating topography, sand, soil, gardens, waterfalls, streams, light prisms, and wind banners encourages children to learn as

they explore. Slides, swings, steps, playhouses, and safety-surface invite interactive play. Built-in flexibility inspires a wide range of new activities and therapies.

Therapies that were perceived as work when they were conducted indoors are now perceived as play when exercised by patients and caregivers in the outdoor PlayGarden. Free from the confines of the rehabilitation hospital, the children eagerly improve their skills, in the fresh air and sunlight.

LANDSCAPE ARCHITECTS AND
THERAPEUTIC PLAY CREATIONS
DESIGNERS
Johansson Design Collaborative Inc., Landscape Architecture (formerly Johansson & Walcavage)

CLIENT TEAM
Nancy Chambers, HTR, Project Manager; with other Rusk therapists

THERAPEUTIC PLAY CREATIONS
ENGINEERS & MANUFACTURERS
Playground Environments International Inc.

TYPE OF FACILITY
Other: Therapeutic Rehabilitation for Children

TYPE OF CONSTRUCTION
New

SITE AREA
.13 acres

TOTAL PROJECT COST
$450,000

STATUS OF PROJECT
Completed September 1998

CONTRACTOR
Padilla Construction Services Inc.

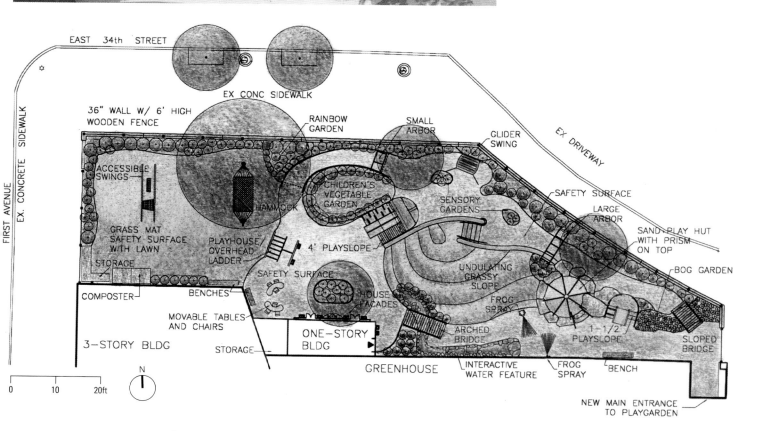

SALISBURY SCHOOL

CITATION

SALISBURY, MARYLAND

ARCHITECT'S STATEMENT

Twenty-five years after creating a primary and middle school for the Salisbury School, our firm was commissioned to design an upper school to extend its programs to grades nine through 12. A modified design-build, our firm created an innovative school design in only 14 months for $95 per square foot. Parents, trustees, faculty, and the headmaster played active roles, participating in workshops to guarantee that the design met the school's aesthetic, financial, and scheduling needs. The new building has an aesthetic similar to the original: open, flexible spaces that facilitate movement from one area to another, communal areas, and residual spaces for chance encounters. At its nexus is a salt dome that houses administration and the library. A classroom building and gymnasium radiate from this hub in a pinwheel configuration, with space for a future fine arts addition. The new facility brings the school into the 21st century: it is fully networked and includes a technology/media center that supports the entire curriculum.

ARCHITECT
**Hardy Holzman Pfeiffer
Associates**

TYPE OF FACILITY
**High School / Innovative
Learning Environment**

TYPE OF CONSTRUCTION
New

SITE AREA
5.3 acres

BUILDING AREA
30,000 square feet

TOTAL PROJECT COST
$4,062,500

STATUS OF PROJECT
Completed 1997

NUMBER OF STUDENTS
150

STRUCTURAL ENGINEER
Davis, Bowen & Friedel, Inc.

CIVIL ENGINEER
Philip Parker Associates

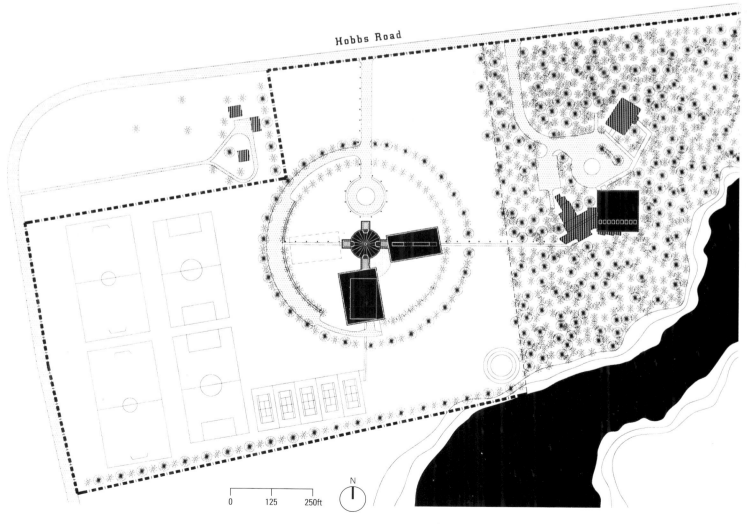

INNOVATIVE LEARNING ENVIRONMENTS

BROWNSBURG CHALLENGER LEARNING CENTER

ARCHITECT'S STATEMENT

Thirteen years ago, the seven heroic Challenger Space Shuttle crew members—sharing a common vision—left behind an incredible legacy. Today, more than half a million students nationally experience that legacy. The mission continues …

In November of 1994, the Brownsburg Community School Corporation dedicated the first Challenger Learning Center in Indiana. Thirty such centers are currently in operation—mostly in museums, science centers, and colleges—across the United States. Brownsburg's center is among only a few nationally which are located within and operated by a public school system.

The Challenger Learning Center is the brainchild of the families of those heroes who died in the Challenger Shuttle mission.

Dr June Scobee Rodgers, a teacher and the widow of Commander Francis R. 'Dick' Scobee, has spearheaded the creation of this living laboratory—a fitting memorial whose mission is to create a positive learning environment that raises students' expectations of success; fosters in them a long-term interest in science, math, and technology; and motivates them to pursue studies in these areas.

ARCHITECT
Schmidt Associates, Inc.

TYPE OF FACILITY
Innovative Learning Environment

TYPE OF CONSTRUCTION
New

BUILDING AREA
9,850 square feet

TOTAL PROJECT COST
$1,224,294

STATUS OF PROJECT
Completed 1994

NUMBER OF STUDENTS
125

STRUCTURAL ENGINEER
Lynch Harrison & Brumleve

MECHANICAL ENGINEER
Schmidt Associates, Inc.

CONTRACTOR
Verkler Inc.

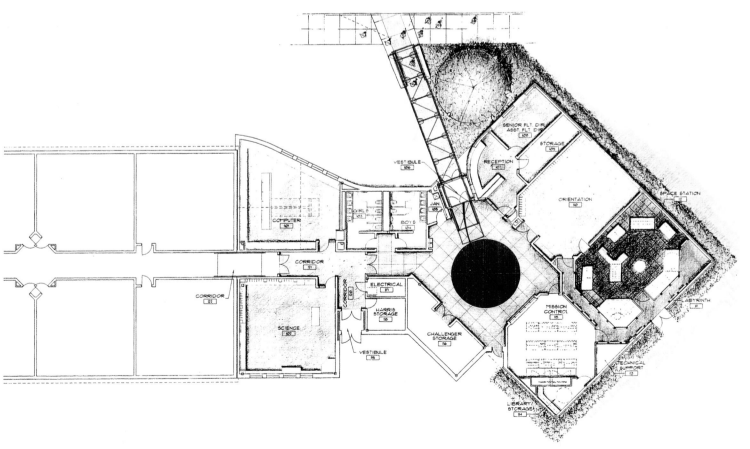

BUILDING BLOCKS MONTESSORI SCHOOL AT THE LEARNING CORRIDOR

ARCHITECT'S STATEMENT

The Building Blocks Montessori School is one of three schools—an elementary, middle, and high school —and a community facility being constructed, simultaneously, as part of The Learning Corridor. It is the centerpiece of a neighborhood revitalization effort championed by Trinity College and being carried out by the Southside Institutions Neighborhood Alliance (SINA) with financial support from the State of Connecticut and the City of Hartford.

The Montessori School is a new 58,000 square foot facility that will serve 320 elementary school-age children from Hartford and surrounding towns.

The design of this magnet school is based on the principles and philosophy of Montessori education. Two stories of classrooms, designed as 'houses for

learning,' are arrayed around an outdoor learning space. All classrooms have easy and direct access to the Learning Center off of an 'interior street' and direct access to the outdoor learning space. Larger assembly, art and music, and recreation spaces are located off the main entrance corridor, and are available for off-hours community use. The school program and design has been reviewed and evaluated by both national and international Montessori educators, and the facility serves as a national model for Montessori school facilities.

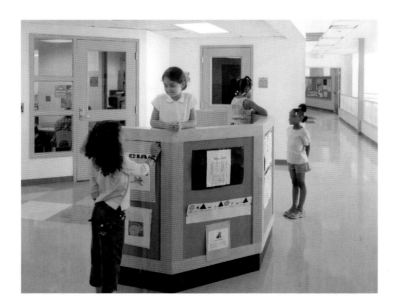

ARCHITECT
Smith Edwards Architects

TYPE OF FACILITY
Early Childhood Learning Environment / Elementary School / Innovative Learning Environment

TYPE OF CONSTRUCTION
New

SITE AREA
2 acres

BUILDING AREA
58,000 square feet

TOTAL PROJECT COST
$9.3 M

STATUS OF PROJECT
Completed 2000

NUMBER OF STUDENTS
320

STRUCTURAL ENGINEER
Macchi Engineers

MECHANICAL ENGINEER
Luchini, Milfort, Goodell & Associates, Inc.

CONTRACTOR
Gilbane Building Co.

THE CENTER FOR APPLIED TECHNOLOGY AND CAREER EXPLORATION

ROCKY MOUNT, VIRGINIA

ARCHITECT'S STATEMENT

Located in a rural southwest Virginia county, this new school exemplifies total community effort: civic leaders, business and industry representatives, local colleges and universities, teachers, parents, school system personnel, and the A/E worked collaboratively to develop the curriculum and the facility. The school consists of eight modules representing career opportunities of the future, including environmental/ natural resources, health and human services, media design, and architectural/ engineering design. Eighth and ninth graders are immersed in real problems and projects, and state-of-the-art technology supports each learning module. The school was designed to simulate a corporate environment, with commons areas, a food court-style cafeteria, modular labs, and an interactive laboratory for teleconferencing. Specific areas of the school, such as the arts and media modules and the teleconference facilities, are shared with the community and local businesses for after hours' use.

Through their experiences at the school, students are receiving first-hand experience in how the corporate world operates. They are developing a work ethic, applying problem-solving skills in diverse collaborative groups, utilizing cutting-edge technology, and devising strategies that will help them adapt to change. This innovative school meets the present-day challenge facing educators to prepare students for the American workforce of the 21st century.

ARCHITECT
HSMM, Inc. (Hayes, Seay, Mattern & Mattern)

TYPE OF FACILITY
Innovative Learning Environment

TYPE OF CONSTRUCTION
New

SITE AREA
15 acres

BUILDING AREA
63,513 square feet

TOTAL PROJECT COST
$8,005,084

STATUS OF PROJECT
Completed 1997

NUMBER OF STUDENTS
400

STRUCTURAL ENGINEER
HSMM

CONTRACTOR
Blair Construction, Inc.

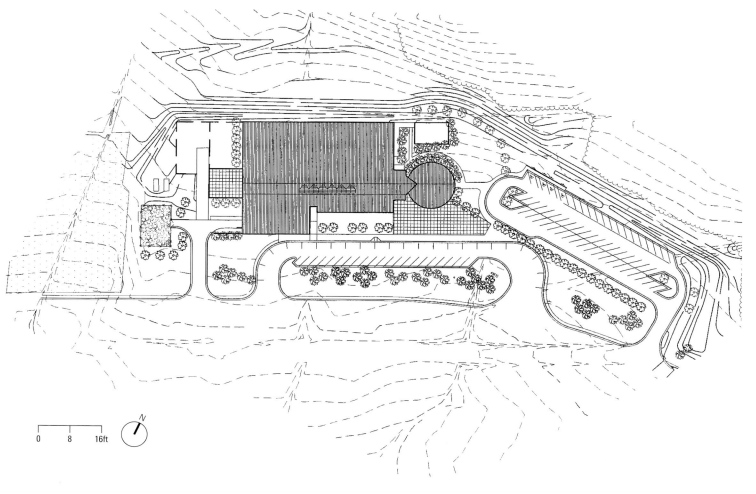

0   8   16ft

N

CHILDREN'S CENTER CAMPUS

KANSAS CITY, MISSOURI

ARCHITECT'S STATEMENT

Three Kansas City organizations sharing similar missions—the YWCA, the Children's Therapeutic Learning Center, and the Children's Center for the Visually Impaired—decided they could better serve the community if they were all under one roof. Such a 'Children's Center Campus' would allow Children's Center TLC and CCVI to share a therapy pool, gym, dining facilities, and administrative space. And the YWCA could provide on-site daycare for children without disabilities, thus helping 'mainstream' children with special needs.

It was important that any such facility be designed to fulfil the distinct programs of each organization. And it was critical that the school be secure but not overly protective, thus preparing children for 'the real world.'

A courtyard concept was chosen to carry out the program. The courtyards naturally meet security needs while giving each organization its own identity. Bright colors and simple geometric forms further distinguish each organization's space. The west façade's brick masonry responds to the surrounding neighborhood while synthetic stucco on the east façade supplies a distinct tactile environment for visually impaired children.

Ultimately, our intention in designing an educational facility that could work effectively in the heart of the city was to enhance the urban community's vitality and viability. The site imposed some constraints that would not have existed in a more suburban location. Nevertheless,

the facility has not only added to the neighborhood, it has also drawn much of its support from the surrounding community. The Children's Center Campus serves as a model of an effective urban presence—architecturally and, more importantly, functionally.

ARCHITECT
BNIM Architects

TYPE OF FACILITY
Innovative Learning Environment

TYPE OF CONSTRUCTION
New

SITE AREA
1.5 acres

BUILDING AREA
50,000 square feet

TOTAL PROJECT COST
$7 M

STATUS OF PROJECT
Completed December 1998

STRUCTURAL ENGINEER
Leigh & O'Kane

MECHANICAL ENGINEER
Henderson Engineering, Inc.

CONTRACTOR
J. E. Dunn Construction Company

EAST VALLEY INSTITUTE OF TECHNOLOGY

MESA, ARIZONA

ARCHITECT'S STATEMENT

In 1990 the voters in 10 school districts in the East Valley approved the formation of a joint technological education district. The new school district was named The East Valley Institute of Technology (EVIT) District #401. The mission of EVIT is to provide a productive, technically trained workforce that meets the market-driven needs of business and industry.

EVIT is a secondary school specializing in a comprehensive curriculum of vocational arts such as photography, business computers, and culinary arts; as well as the manual arts such as construction, machine technology, and auto mechanics.

EVIT administrators conducted the facility programming process, with the assistance of the BPLW Planning Division. During the preparation of the Campus Facility Program a participatory planning process was used that began by collecting all relevant information regarding the facilities and the programs of the school. The information was augmented by review of questionnaires completed by key personnel, on-site interviews, and evaluation of the programs and facilities. The planning team then presented it to the committee for review and direction. The campus consists of 11 buildings, totaling 317,000 square feet.

ARCHITECT
BPLW Architects & Engineers, Inc.

TYPE OF FACILITY
Innovative Learning Environment

TYPE OF CONSTRUCTION
New/Renovation

SITE AREA
75 acres

BUILDING AREA
317,000 square feet

TOTAL PROJECT COST
$40,853,203

STATUS OF PROJECT
Completed 1998

NUMBER OF STUDENTS
6,000

STRUCTURAL ENGINEER
Caruso, Turley & Scott

MECHANICAL ENGINEER
LSW Engineers

CONTRACTOR
Slettin Construction Co.

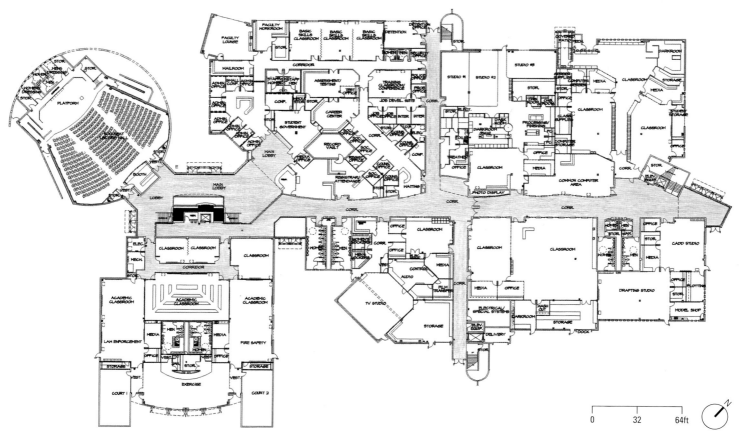

0   32   64ft

INNOVATIVE LEARNING ENVIRONMENTS

GENKO UCHIDA BUILDING

ARCHITECT'S STATEMENT

The project provides state-of-the-art high-tech music learning environments in a student-centered facility. The contemporary music school, with over 2,900 students, needed maximum expansion of its teaching resources, which failed to meet current acoustic and technological standards. Two newly purchased historic structures offered the opportunity to define and satisfy top-priority program space demands, and to accommodate intense student learning style, academic support, and administrative service needs. Key aspects include:

- Interactive planning process: Architects worked for six months with a representative 30-member working group of faculty, students, and administrators to review all current academic and administrative space use, identify priority space needs and characteristics, and test alternative space reallocation models and designs.

- Complex facility program: 200-seat multipurpose performance hall/function space; three large rehearsal classrooms; six ensemble workshops; 10 guitar labs; five percussion labs; four piano labs; practice rooms; private lesson studios; guitar, percussion, and ensemble department offices; admissions, career resources, counseling; financial, community, and student affairs offices; student lounge and computer lab.

- Historic buildings and district challenge: The site, in a historic district with strict design guidelines, had a 32,000 square foot, five-story concrete-frame 1910-vintage automobile dealership with inappropriate 1970's glazed-brick-and-strip-window façade, and an 8,500 square foot townhouse from 1903. We worked for one and a half years with Historic District Commission, City

Planning Agency, local neighborhood, and commercial associations through multiple site development, massing, and exterior treatment schemes to achieve 'the most successful new edifice to be built in the commercial district in a very long time.'

- Contemporary teaching facility in a traditional shell: Our design concept maximizes capacity with a unified three-part complex: 1. Gutting auto dealership to its structural frame, removing the roof and adding a top floor, stripping the façade and replacing with brick-and-limestone compatible with its traditional neighbors. 2. Restoring brick townhouse exterior and renovating the interior for smaller-scale student affairs, lounge, computer lab, and offices. 3. Seven-story addition behind the townhouse, floor levels matching the main building, for

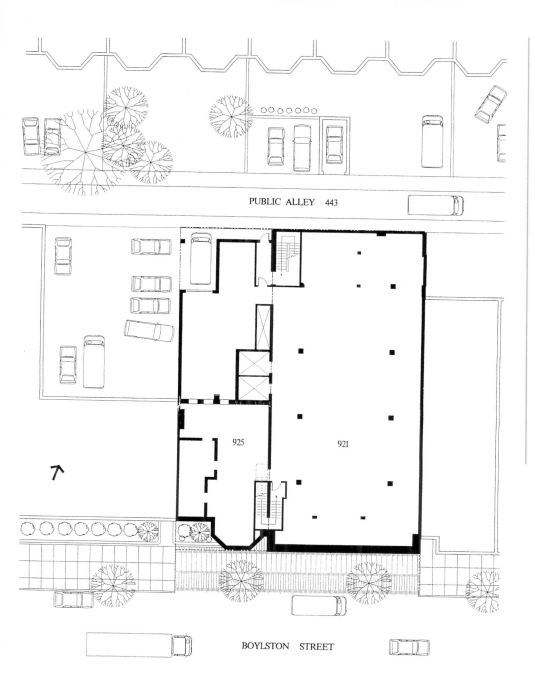

PUBLIC ALLEY 443

925　　921

BOYLSTON STREET

ARCHITECT
Miller Dyer Spears Inc.

TYPE OF FACILITY
Innovative Learning Environment

TYPE OF CONSTRUCTION
Addition/Renovation

SITE AREA
9,100 square feet

BUILDING AREA
58,000 square feet

TOTAL PROJECT COST
$12 M

STATUS OF PROJECT
Completed 1997

NUMBER OF STUDENTS
2,900

STRUCTURAL ENGINEER
Souza, True & Partners, Inc.

MECHANICAL/ELECTRICAL
ENGINEER
TMP Consulting Engineers, Inc.

CONTRACTOR
Shawmut Design & Construction, Inc.

more music teaching, community affairs, admininistration, and service space. The three components are connected and integrated at all floors, with new elevators and service core at the joint, for full accessibility.

• Vibrant mix of music and student spaces: Diverse performance, teaching, student activities, and administration functions, intermixed throughout the complex, give students and visitors a taste of the school's vital life and broad offerings. Interior glazing opens views from hallways into all class and activity spaces.

• Flexible performance hall: Semi-circular, balconied 200-seat hall, carved from the concrete frame, with loose seating and segmented, movable wooden stage to accommodate large and small

ensembles, concerts 'in-the-round,' and receptions. Sliding-panel acoustically sealed doors open to the lobby for expanded capacity. Room acoustics and shape, wood-paneled stage, movable drapes and screens effectively accommodate both electronic and non-amplified music.

• Networked digital audio system: All classrooms, labs, rehearsal, and performance facilities are networked to a real-time, fully digitized music audio resource system, and are equipped with the latest audio-visual and acoustic technology, and with computer-projection and recording-studio sound-control capability in the hall.

HARFORD GLEN ENVIRONMENTAL EDUCATION CENTER

HARFORD COUNTY, MARYLAND

ARCHITECT'S STATEMENT

The Harford Glen Environmental Education Center is a 269 acre park of forested hills and a marshy reservoir surrounded by suburban residential development. Existing buildings date to the 1800s. The 'Mansion House' serves as administration, classroom, and museum space. The natural setting is a wildlife sanctuary to hundreds of animals and provides an ideal surrounding for first-hand environmental studies.

Fifth-graders spend one week in-residence at Harford Glen. The primary needs of this Phase II development are facilities to increase the student capacity and extend the season of operation.

The response is two new dormitory/classroom buildings, a multipurpose classroom building, and pavilion in conformance with a 1993 master plan.

The buildings provide a campus-like link between the Mansion House and the dining hall. Each classroom incorporates an overhead door for indoor/outdoor activities under the deep canopies. The pavilion is sized for total group assembly. The dormitory levels are divided into wings with teachers' rooms for supervision.

The design was developed over a seven-month period with the continued input of a design committee. Construction was completed in seven months.

ARCHITECT
Banta Campbell Architects, Inc.

TYPE OF FACILITY
**Elementary School / Innovative
Learning Environment**

TYPE OF CONSTRUCTION
New

SITE AREA
269 acres

BUILDING AREA
20,032 square feet

TOTAL PROJECT COST
$1,613,355

STATUS OF PROJECT
Completed February 1998

NUMBER OF STUDENTS
125

STRUCTURAL ENGINEER
**Alison, McCormac &
Nickolaus/Columbia Engineers, Inc.**

MECHANICAL/ELECTRICAL
ENGINEER
Phoenix Design Group Ltd

CONTRACTOR
Jack H. Kidd Associates

1. CLASSROOM / DORMITORY BUILDING
2. CLASSROOM / DORMITORY BUILDING
3. OUTDOOR COVERED PAVILION
4. MULTI-PURPOSE BUILDING
5. KITCHEN / DINING HALL REPLACEMENT (1999)
6. MANSION HOUSE
7. ICE HOUSE
8. CORN CRIB
9. CAMPFIRE / OUTDOOR CLASSROOM
10. BEAVER LODGE
11. PARKING
12. ENTRY DRIVE
13. RESERVOIR

0   100   200ft

N

LakeView Technology Academy

ARCHITECT'S STATEMENT

Made possible through a collaboration between the K–12 school district, local colleges, and the business community, this school will provide students with a unique opportunity to graduate from high school with a strong emphasis in manufacturing and engineering technology. The same facility that educates high school students by day will provide evening classes for college students, training and retraining for workers employed by many of the Kenosha area manufacturing facilities, and adults looking to gain the skills to secure a job in manufacturing.

The academy provides a collaborative, multi-disciplinary, combined career/college prep approach to high school education. Course work in math, communications,

science, technology, and manufacturing processes is coordinated into a program that encourages and enables students to apply the facts and concepts that are being taught. Teamwork and communication are an integral part of all classes.

Classroom spaces of the school provide separate teaching areas in a nontraditional, open, office-like setting. Each year 110 new ninth graders choose to enter this innovative, dynamic program. The program serves a total of 440 students, grades 9–12.

ARCHITECT
**Partners in Design
Architects, Inc.**

TYPE OF FACILITY
**High School / Innovative
Learning Environment /
Corporate or Other
Specialized Center**

TYPE OF CONSTRUCTION
New

SITE AREA
9.29 acres

BUILDING AREA
40,000 square feet

TOTAL PROJECT COST
$3,569,000

STATUS OF PROJECT
Completed 1999

NUMBER OF STUDENTS
440

STRUCTURAL ENGINEER
R.C. Schend & Associates

MECHANICAL ENGINEER
George Uttech

ELECTRICAL ENGINEER
Speaker Electric

CONTRACTOR
Riley Construction

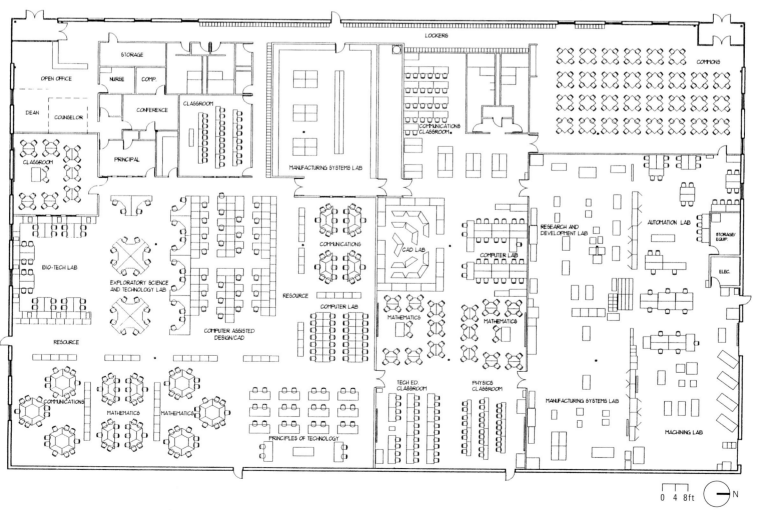

MeySen Academy, Kamiyagari Campus

Architect's statement

The design of this project grew out of the unique circumstances of MeySen Academy, and the culture and the site of which it is part.

Founded over 30 years ago by expatriate Americans, MeySen provides early childhood education and after-school elementary-level English language and other programs. The school has Japanese and American faculty and staff; the student body is typically Japanese.

Primary goals included:

- Create a school facility that reflects and supports the unique American/Japanese bi-cultural tradition of MeySen Academy.

- Provide a 'welcoming' atmosphere to facilitate the child's transition from home to school and broader community beyond.

- Preserve valuable open space and landscape features, and integrate the buildings into the park-like campus setting.

- Reflect the educational philosophies and building traditions of the two cultures in the physical environment.

- The architectural vocabulary makes reference to both Japanese and American building traditions. 'Residential' qualities were incorporated to create a relaxed atmosphere and provide a contrast to the institutional image of a 'typical' Japanese school. To maintain a scale appropriate to the park-like setting, second-floor classrooms were integrated into the roof structure and provided with dormer windows.

- Each classroom has a 'corner' location to provide the room with daylight on two sides and to allow for cross-ventilation.

All classrooms share a common interior area, which is used for a variety of purposes.

The design and construction of this project was a collaborative effort between Japanese and American teams. Tours of educational facilities in Japan and the United States provided a valuable basis for comparison and improved the understanding of the differences and similarities of the two traditions. Both Japanese and American building materials were utilized in the construction.

ARCHITECT
Michael Whalen, AIA; Hazama Corporation

TYPE OF FACILITY
Early Childhood Learning Environment / Elementary School

TYPE OF CONSTRUCTION
New

SITE AREA
8 acres

BUILDING AREA
31,000 square feet

STATUS OF PROJECT
Completed 1999

NUMBER OF STUDENTS
1,500

STRUCTURAL/MECHANICAL/
ELECTRICAL ENGINEER
Hazama Corporation

CONTRACTOR
Hazama Corporation

CONSTRUCTION MANAGER
Tsuji Management Inc.

NEAL SMITH NATIONAL WILDLIFE REFUGE PRAIRIE LEARNING CENTER

PRAIRIE CITY, IOWA

ARCHITECT'S STATEMENT

Primary needs/goals:

- Environmental education
  Provide innovative on-site and outreach programming for a variety of audiences with an emphasis on developing an awareness and appreciation of conservation.

- Research
  Provide research opportunities to support habitat reconstruction and restoration. Document the tallgrass prairie reconstruction and restoration process in a scientific format.

- Interpretation and recreation
  Provide opportunities for the public to understand and enjoy wildlife and wildland resources.

Design process:

- Introductory seminars were organized by the Service to educate the design team about the prairie ecosystem, history, biodiversity, current research, prairie maintenance, and environmental education.

- Visits to neighboring cultural facilities close to refuge.

- Visits to exemplary visitor centers across the US to assess strengths and weaknesses relative to this facility's purposes and goals.

- Environmental Education/Interpretation Workshops were organized to:

  Brainstorm important messages, story ideas, content structures, and delivery approaches.

Create several alternative storylines, exhibit concepts, and exhibit space layouts.

Analyze alternatives and select and refine final exhibit concepts.

- Exhibit designer worked collaboratively from the beginning to develop stories and develop space adjacencies and sizes for the facility.

- Presentation by theatre group to explore story-telling, programming, and participatory involvement as an education tool.

- Presentation by video group to explore media for video scenes for different seasons and stories of the prairie.

ADA consultant lecture provided awareness of handicapped accessibility and seamless shared access. Reviewed final designs for compliance and incorporation of ideas.

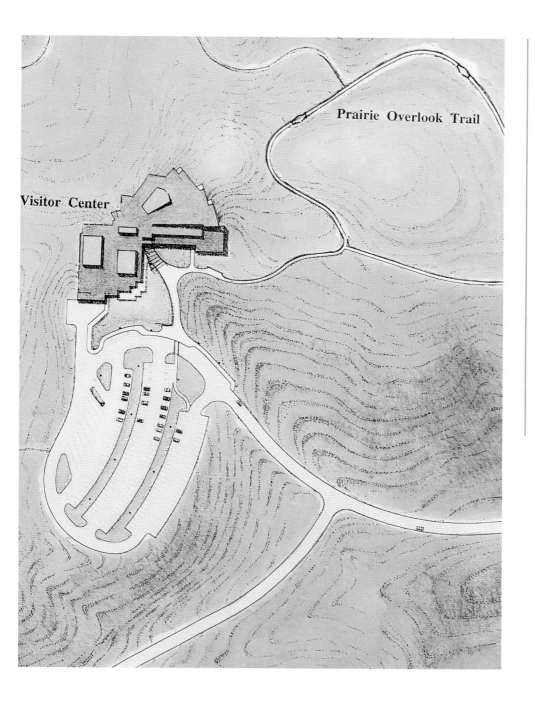

Prairie Overlook Trail

Visitor Center

ARCHITECT
OZ Architecture

TYPE OF FACILITY
Innovative Learning Environment

TYPE OF CONSTRUCTION
New

SITE AREA
8,000 acres

BUILDING AREA
20,000 square feet

TOTAL PROJECT COST
$21,850,000

STATUS OF PROJECT
Completed 1996 / Exhibitry 1997

STRUCTURAL ENGINEER
Martin Martin

MECHANICAL ENGINEER
Gordon Gumeson

CONTRACTOR
Taylor Ball

TRAVIS L. WILLIAMS
FAMILY SERVICES CENTER

ARCHITECT'S STATEMENT

This Family Services & Learning Center is projected to service 7,200 families annually within an inner city community that is searching for the catalyst to improve its neighborhoods and outlook. The center, with its wide range of programs, is intended to be that catalyst. Educational offerings provide proactive measures and opportunities to all generations of the community.

In this facility, learning is equated with hope. The massing and configuration of this new structure is designed to cultivate community optimism. The bow trusses, which clear-span the main wings of the building, are shaped like an air-foil, providing an uplifting character to the center. A multitude of functions are housed in these wings. They are grouped under the air-foil form, with emphasis given to the overall volume, symbolizing that each program is a part of a greater whole, part of the community.

The wings of the building reach out to the surrounding neighborhoods and offer an inviting courtyard surrounding the entry lobby. This courtyard literally radiates out toward its neighbors, focusing both pedestrians and motorists upon the center's presence and the opportunity it represents.

ARCHITECT
Gabor Lorant Architects Inc.

TYPE OF FACILITY
**Early Childhood Learning
Environment / Innovative
Learning Environment / Other
or Multipurpose**

TYPE OF CONSTRUCTION
New

SITE AREA
3.39 acres

BUILDING AREA
20,250 square feet

TOTAL PROJECT COST
$2,712,000

STATUS OF PROJECT
Completed September 1999

NUMBER OF STUDENTS
1,400

LANDSCAPE ARCHITECTS
Logan Simpson Design Inc.

STRUCTURAL ENGINEER
KPFF Consulting Engineers

MECHANICAL/ELECTRICAL
ENGINEER
NP Mechanical Inc.

CIVIL ENGINEER
EEC/MKE

GEOTECHNICAL ENGINEERS
Speedie & Associates

CONTRACTOR
Brignall Construction

WALNUT HILLS ARTS & SCIENCE CENTER

CINCINNATI, OHIO

ARCHITECT'S STATEMENT

When plans began developing for a new Arts and Science Center, they started with the school's core principles—a classical curriculum and educational excellence. Designers met with faculty, students, administrators, parents, and alumni to understand their values. They also met with faculty at leading academic institutions to learn more about the best practices in the design of science and arts facilities. From this research, six main themes developed:

- enhanced experiential learning
- indoor–outdoor learning
- enhanced interdisciplinary learning
- advanced access to technology
- architectural harmony
- flexibility.

The building's architecture reflects the school's strong tradition in academics and profound respect for history with an eye toward the future. Every learning space is wired for full voice, video, and data accessibility. To increase hands-on learning opportunities, laboratory space was increased in size and count, including a large scientific workshop where major projects can be developed. An innovative science courtyard provides an on site, natural living environment for students to study. A sculpture courtyard enables the creation and display of large art works the whole school can experience. By combining art, science, and math programs into one facility, cross-curriculum opportunities increase and interdisciplinary learning comes to life.

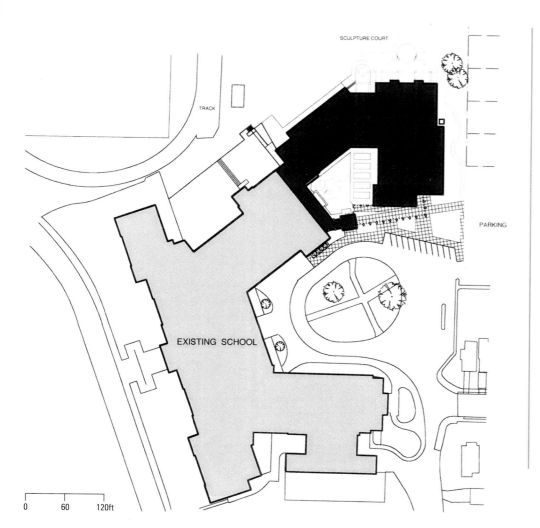

SCULPTURE COURT

TRACK

EXISTING SCHOOL

PARKING

0   60   120ft

ARCHITECT
Steed Hammond Paul Inc.

TYPE OF FACILITY
High School / Innovative Learning Environment

TYPE OF CONSTRUCTION
Addition/Renovation

SITE AREA
2 acres

BUILDING AREA
59,000 square feet

TOTAL PROJECT COST
$8 M

STATUS OF PROJECT
Completed December 1999

NUMBER OF STUDENTS
2,100

STRUCTURAL ENGINEER
Graham, Obermeyer and Partners, Ltd.

MECHANICAL/ELECTRICAL ENGINEER
Motz Consulting Engineers, Inc.

CONTRACTOR
BBL-Maescher

INNOVATIVE LEARNING ENVIRONMENTS

WISDOM HALL, ANTIOCH COMMUNITY HIGH SCHOOL DISTRICT 117

ANTIOCH, ILLINOIS

ARCHITECT'S STATEMENT

A high school Learning Assistance Program (LAP) required space that enhances the abilities of students who need help learning how to learn. The renovated Wisdom Hall allows students with different learning styles to embrace their differences and to use their time to study in the manner best suited for them.

Approaching the project, the team met with LAP staff to identify program needs, compiling a list of essential elements. To address the divergent needs of auditory, visual, multi-sensory, and independent learners within 2,750 square feet, architects created distinct learning zones, each

serving multiple intelligences. Learning areas comprise individual study, one-on-one work, small group events, computer-based activities, large group sessions, and a project area. Staff is present to assess, assist, and guide the learner.

The project was designed inexpensively, costing just $39 per square foot, including fixtures, furnishings, and equipment. Because the space assigned to the program by the school district was a small one, designers had to use walls, colors, furniture, and materials to accommodate program needs and to make the space an intimate, inviting learning environment.

ARCHITECT
OWP&P, Chicago, Illinois

TYPE OF FACILITY
High School / Innovative Learning Environment

TYPE OF CONSTRUCTION
Renovation

BUILDING AREA
2,750 square feet

TOTAL PROJECT COST
$59,209

STATUS OF PROJECT
Completed 1996

NUMBER OF STUDENTS
67 (Wisdom Hall); 1,950 (total school)

STRUCTURAL/MECHANICAL/ ELECTRICAL ENGINEER
OWP&P

CONTRACTOR
Seater Construction Company

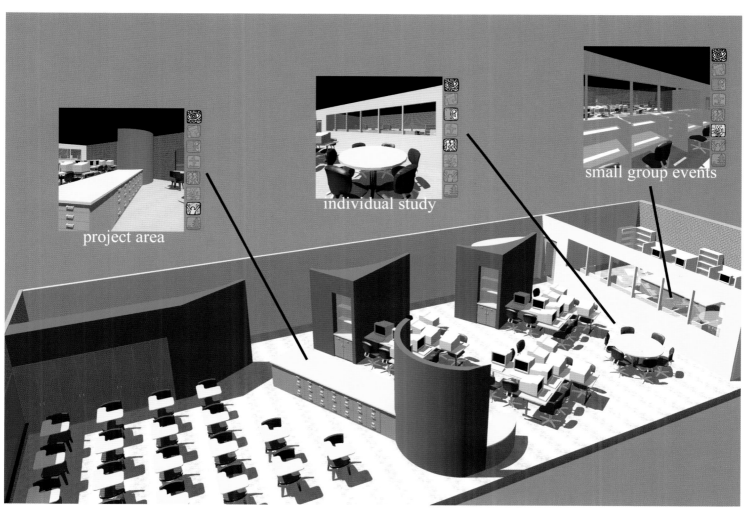

project area

individual study

small group events

FACILITIES

EDUCATIONAL

TWO-YEAR TECHNICAL OR COMMUNITY COLLEGES

BOROUGH OF MANHATTAN COMMUNITY COLLEGE

MERIT

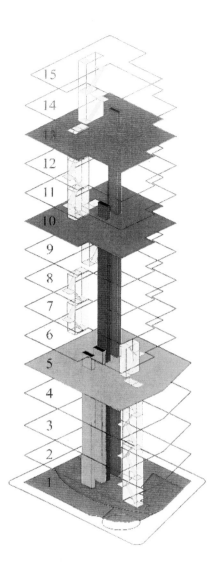

ARCHITECT'S STATEMENT

When a 1959 office building was donated to the Borough of Manhattan Community College, it provided this urban college an opportunity not only to relieve severe overcrowding on its campus, but create a state-of-the-art academic building for its students. Working closely with the academic and administrative deans and faculty members, a design resulted that will meet the needs of students, teachers, and the surrounding community well into the 21st century.

The building will be fully wired for computer-based learning, a 24-hour virtual library will provide students with vast online resources, and a pre-K through second grade school will serve children of students and the community.

A new two-story entrance with student lounges, an art gallery, café, and other amenities enlivens the streetscape and asserts the building's new identity as a place for higher learning and career development.

In keeping with its mission to serve the surrounding business community, state-of-the-art classrooms will be used by neighboring financial institutions for staff training. One floor is transformed into an incubator for hi-tech, start-up companies, providing struggling entrepreneurs with needed resources and students with real-life learning opportunities and marketable skills.

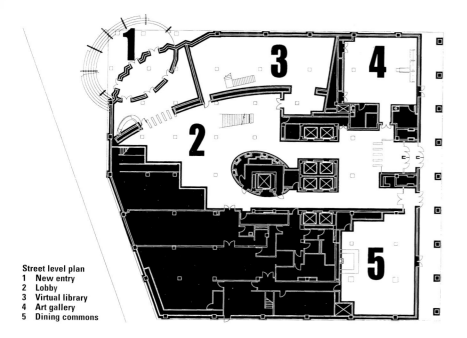

Street level plan
1 New entry
2 Lobby
3 Virtual library
4 Art gallery
5 Dining commons

ARCHITECT
Hardy Holzman Pfeiffer Associates

TYPE OF FACILITY
Two-year Technical or Community College

TYPE OF CONSTRUCTION
Renovation

SITE AREA
1/2 acre

BUILDING AREA
360,000 square feet

TOTAL PROJECT COST
$62 M

STATUS OF PROJECT
Estimated completion date October 2001

NUMBER OF STUDENTS
7,200

STRUCTURAL ENGINEER
Weiskopf & Pickworth

MECHANICAL/ELECTRICAL/ PLUMBING ENGINEER
Altieri Sebor Wieber

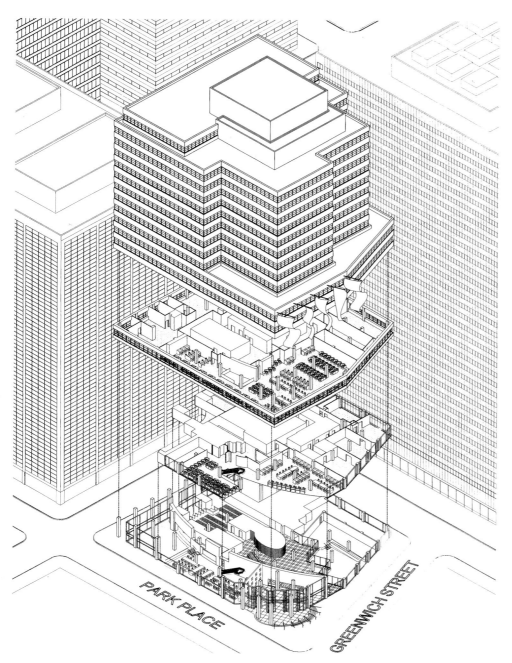

CENTER FOR INTERACTIVE LEARNING

DAYTON, OHIO

ARCHITECT'S STATEMENT

This cutting-edge educational facility is a place where people of diverse backgrounds can see and experience the future of learning and work. The building facilitates the college's goal of equipping students with the skills required to succeed in the rapidly changing, technology-driven workplace.

The design is an effective response to the need for flexible space that accommodates annual changes in curriculum and provides accessibility to current and unknown future technology.

Two of the building's most dynamic areas are the Cyber Tree and the Forum. The Cyber Tree extends form the lower level to the ceiling's virtual skylight and contains interactive exhibits on each level. These exhibits serve as an orientation and informational resource for students and visitors.

The 90-seat Forum is a multi-level theatre and seminar room that features three floor-to-ceiling projections screens, surround sound and theatrical lighting, and technology that offers internal and external linkages.

Since the building opened in September 1998, students and professors have found this compelling invitation to experience technology captivating and energizing. Accordingly, attendance is up and expectations are growing.

ARCHITECT
Lorenz + Williams Incorporated

TYPE OF FACILITY
Two-year Technical or Community College

TYPE OF CONSTRUCTION
New

SITE AREA
2 acres

BUILDING AREA
75,000 square feet

TOTAL PROJECT COST
$27.4 M

STATUS OF PROJECT
Completed 1998

NUMBER OF STUDENTS
19,999

STRUCTURAL ENGINEER
THP Limited

MECHANICAL ENGINEER
Stan and Associates, Inc.

ELECTRICAL ENGINEER
Progressive Engineering

CONTRACTOR
Turner Construction

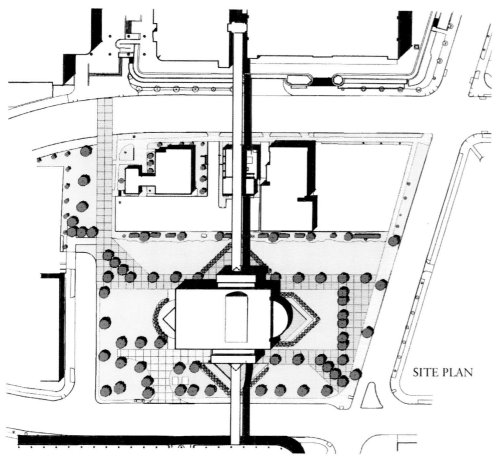

SITE PLAN

CENTRE DE FORMATION PROFESSIONNELLE ÉLECTROTECHNIQUE ET MACHINE FIXE

QUÉBEC, CANADA

ARCHITECT'S STATEMENT

The project involved the creation of teaching spaces to provide practical experience in technical skills. The design reflects the two facets of the school's curriculum: teaching maintenance of building power plant machinery, and technologies related to running factories (electronics, hydraulics, mechanics, and pneumatics).

Simulations of typical working environments are provided as stage sets for learning. These teaching spaces also respond to the changing needs of evolving technologies. This is, to our knowledge, the first facility of its kind.

The program required the expansion and reorganization of existing facilities. The design committee consisted of teaching staff as well as the design architects and engineers. Three-dimensional sketches and models were used to represent the spaces, their equipment, and the building that encloses them.

Costs were controlled during the design process by progressive cost-benefit analysis. The construction was carefully planned to avoid interruption of educational programs; in fact, not a single hour of instruction was lost.

All the functional relationships were approved by a teaching team. Their input was essential in concept development, and more particularly in the coming-together of ideas which led to the final design.

ARCHITECT
**Régis Côté et associés /
Marcel Valin, architectes**

TYPE OF FACILITY
**Two-year Technical or
Community College**

TYPE OF CONSTRUCTION
Addition/Renovation

SITE AREA
6.548 acres

TOTAL PROJECT COST
$5,976,987

STATUS OF PROJECT
Completed 1999

NUMBER OF STUDENTS
495

STRUCTURAL ENGINEER
Genium

MECHANICAL/ELECTRICAL
ENGINEER
Genivar

CONTRACTOR
Les Entreprises Québechab inc.

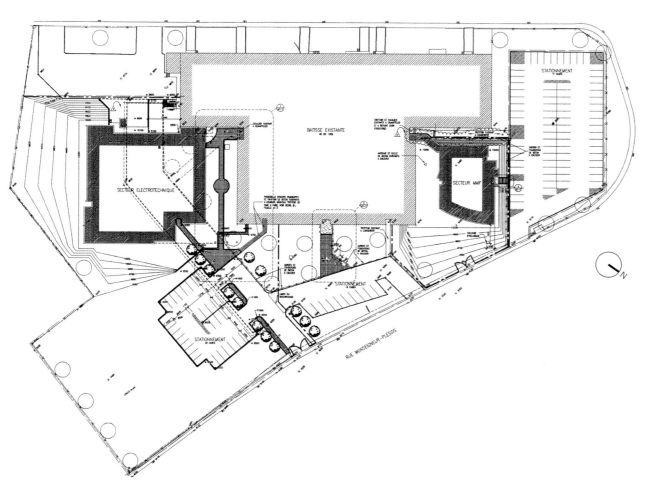

DECKER HEALTH SCIENCES BUILDING

ARCHITECT'S STATEMENT

The Decker Health Sciences Building is a new 68,000 square foot building that will contain the various departments of the Broome Community College Health Sciences Division. The building is the first new structure built under the new Master Plan Guidelines that were developed by the same architect in an earlier phase. It was determined that the campus needed to consolidate all of its allied health science programs to one location. The building brings together all these departments previously scattered throughout the campus. Each of the relocated departments is being expanded to meet the goals as projected in the master plan. During the master plan process, dental clinic faculty and members of the college administration were interviewed to shape the components of the program. The seven major departments include nursing, dental hygiene, medical laboratory technology,

physical and occupational therapy, medical assistant, radiology technology, and health information technology. Laboratory, classroom, and faculty environments for all of these have been provided and the building contains a large dental clinic open to the public, which is part of the dental hygienists' program.

In addition to the seven departments, the new facility contains common areas including administrative offices, classrooms, a new Learning Resource Center, student lounges, and a large lecture hall. The lecture hall and its adjacent spaces will serve campus-wide educational functions as well as gatherings of the community surrounding the campus. The building was occupied in 1998 with post-occupancy review taking place the year after.

The location and massing for the building stemmed from the campus master plan as well. Another major change to the campus formulated in the master plan is the creation of a new entrance to the college. Due to changes in the road system and other building projects adjacent to the campus, it was determined to shift the student entrance on campus from the east to the south. The Decker Health Sciences Building forms half of the new entrance gateway from the parking areas to the heart of the campus.

The parking lots for this commuter campus were re-planned and modified to a series of radical lots. These parking areas are a full story below the elevation of the existing academic quadrangle and the new Decker Health Sciences Building mitigates between these two elevations. The building mass is organized into two wings separated by a

ARCHITECT
Perkins Eastman Architects PC

TYPE OF FACILITY
Two-year Technical or Community College

TYPE OF CONSTRUCTION
New

SITE AREA
220 acres

BUILDING AREA
72,000 square feet

TOTAL PROJECT COST
$10 M

STATUS OF PROJECT
Completed January 1998

NUMBER OF STUDENTS
5,200

STRUCTURAL/MECHANICAL/
ELECTRICAL ENGINEER
McFarland-Johnson

CONTRACTORS
Daniel J. Lynch Inc.; James L. Lewis, Inc.; Panko Electric; Piccirilli Slavik and Vincent

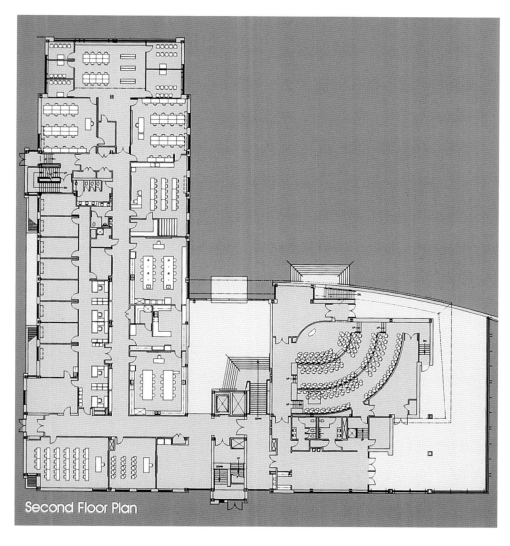

Second Floor Plan

two-story entrance lobby allowing entrance from both the parking elevation and the quadrangle elevation. The northern three-story wing faces the parking to the south and the college quadrangles to the north. The eastern end of this wing is a monumental exterior granite stairway. The southern two-story wing faces parking to the east and playing fields to the west. This wing houses the public dental clinic with its own separate entrance on the first floor. On the second floor is a large, tiered multipurpose lecture hall for use by the entire community for special events. This room leads to an outdoor roof terrace, which is also accessed by an exterior stairway from the ground floor entrance plaza.

The original campus was built in the 1950s as a science and technology campus. Most of the buildings were built of brick and precast concrete with colored metal spandrel common to that era. The Decker Health Science Building uses compatible brick materials and metals in a somewhat different vocabulary. The lobby tower houses one of the major stairways and mechanical penthouses offering the campus an identifiable icon.

DES MOINES AREA COMMUNITY COLLEGE— NEWTON POLYTECHNIC CAMPUS

NEWTON, IOWA

ARCHITECT'S STATEMENT

A Fortune 500-rated appliance manufacturer, headquartered in a mid-sized midwest community, declared a warehouse on its corporate campus a surplus property. In four short months, corporate executives, along with leaders from an area community college and the city itself, structured a deal that would finance the transformation of the warehouse into a center for learning.

This unique alliance blends private and public interests. Educational spaces are organized along an 'educational mall' circulation spine (main street), which allows for integration of all types of learners as well as flexible expansion of new programs and new alliance members.

The facility currently accommodates space for:

- continuing adult education programs
- alternative high school programs
- technical training laboratories for the Maytag Corporation
- full-service conference center and auditorium
- labs and electronic classrooms linked to the ICN (statewide fiber optic network)
- extension opportunities that now include Masters programs through two major state universities.

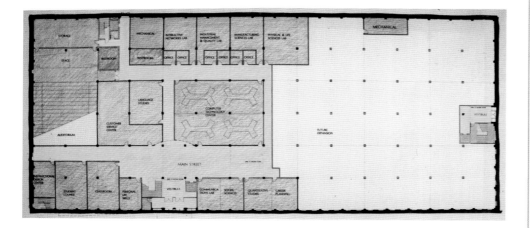

ARCHITECT
RDG Bussard Dikis Inc.

TYPE OF FACILITY
Alternative School / Innovative Learning Environment / Two-year Technical or Community College / Corporate or Other Specialized Training Center

TYPE OF CONSTRUCTION
Renovation

SITE AREA
5.3 acres

BUILDING AREA
102,883 square feet

TOTAL PROJECT COST
$5,282,848

STATUS OF PROJECT
Completed 1993

STRUCTURAL ENGINEER
Dennis & Magnani

MECHANICAL ENGINEER
The Waldinger Corporation

ELECTRICAL ENGINEER
Brown Brothers

CONTRACTOR
The Alter Design Build Group

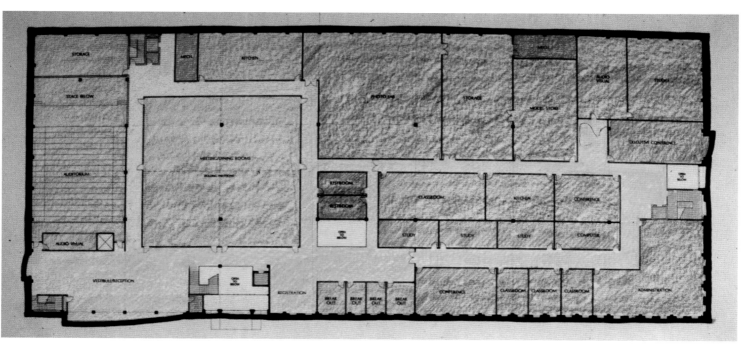

GLENDALE CAMPUS, NIAGARA COLLEGE CANADA

ONTARIO, CANADA

ARCHITECT'S STATEMENT

The program for this project was for a full-service college campus including a state-of-the-art learning resource center, a student services center, a 240-seat auditorium, gymnasium, and cafetorium. Enrolment at the new campus includes 2,500 full-time day students and 12,000 students in continuing education. Program offerings specialize in business, integrated manufacturing technologies, and horticultural and environmental training.

This project, primarily funded by the provincial government, represents the first major capital expansion at the college since its inception in 1967. Realizing that this project represented an opportunity not to be available again, the college administration, under the guidance of the Board of Governors, crafted a series of 'guiding principles' to ensure that the new facility would respond to the future demands of post-secondary education.

The project dealt not only with the design and construction of a new campus facility, but also with how the college would best deliver its services. This allowed ideally for the design of the building to be forged in conjunction with an improved management structure and operational plan.

The design process was driven through a master Plan Development Committee that included the president, the vice presidents, the college's project manager, the director of physical resources, the architects' representative, and the cost consultant. The involvement of senior level staff at all key stages of the program planning and design stages allowed the team to resolve issues openly and quickly.

This unique approach provided the design team with the advantage of a simple, direct, and efficient decision-making

process, which was a tremendous benefit to the project schedule. The approach has also maintained the project's vision through a one-year suspension in the project, changes in curriculum, and changes within the senior administration of the college itself.

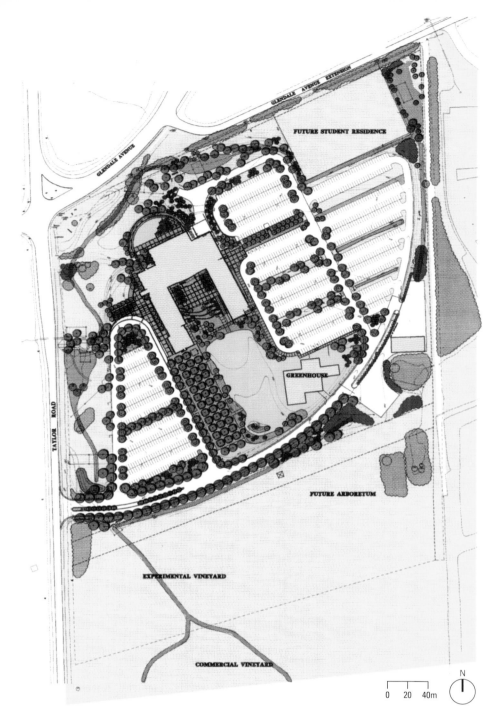

ARCHITECT
Moffat Kinoshita Architects

TYPE OF FACILITY
Two-year Technical or Community College

TYPE OF CONSTRUCTION
New

SITE AREA
50 acres

BUILDING AREA
218,000 square feet

TOTAL PROJECT COST
$35.8 M

STATUS OF PROJECT
Completed September 1998

NUMBER OF STUDENTS
2,500

STRUCTURAL ENGINEER
Halsall & Associates Ltd.

MECHANICAL ENGINEER
Group Eight Engineering Limited

CONTRACTOR
Bondfield Construction Company (1983) Limited

GLENDALE COMMUNITY COLLEGE APPLIED SCIENCES TEACHING LAB

GLENDALE, ARIZONA

ARCHITECT'S STATEMENT

The building is organized to maximize the use of exterior circulation and access to natural light. Day-lit perimeter labs flank the lab prep and service core, allowing for a clear separation of student and staff circulation. The support zone also serves as the distribution core for utilities to each of the labs fed from mechanical and electrical rooms at the east and west ends of the building. Separation of chemistry labs permits the optimization of the air handling and lab services for each wing.

The student commons/faculty offices serve as the central hub of the building; faculty offices are organized in a series of volumes within this open day-lit area adjacent to the student study areas and lecture halls. Display and exhibits occupy this area to encourage student and faculty interaction.

The architecture is inspired by the existing campus vocabulary, interpreting elements by responding to color, form, and texture with the materials intrinsic in the new building. Exposed concrete tilt slab and masonry walls are used in combination with ground concrete floors and exposed steel structure to express the tectonic nature of the building.

ARCHITECT
Richard & Bauer Architecture LLC

TYPE OF FACILITY
Community College

TYPE OF CONSTRUCTION
New

SITE AREA
3.1 acres

BUILDING AREA
33,800 square feet

TOTAL PROJECT COST
$4.8 M

STATUS OF PROJECT
Completed June 2000

NUMBER OF STUDENTS
530

STRUCTURAL ENGINEER
Caruso Turley Scott Inc.

MECHANICAL/ELECTRICAL
ENGINEER
GLHN Engineers

CONTRACTOR
Sun Eagle Corporation

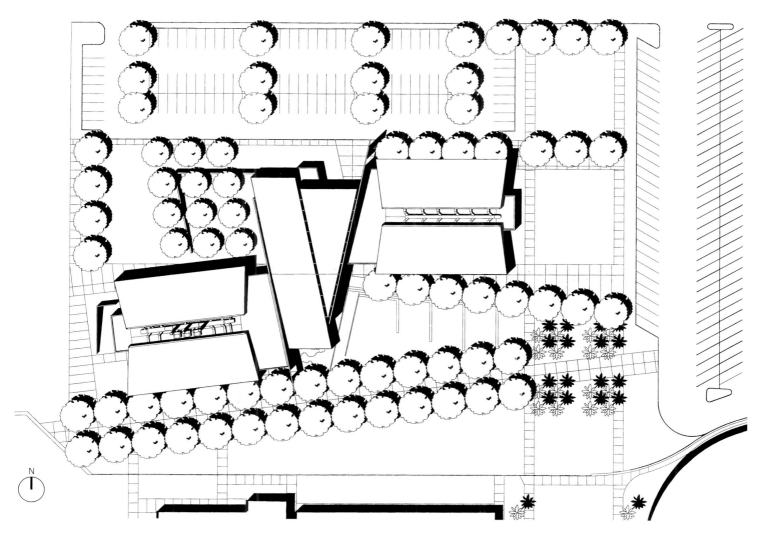

N

STUDENT SUPPORT SERVICES, PARADISE VALLEY COMMUNITY COLLEGE

PHOENIX, ARIZONA

ARCHITECT'S STATEMENT

The Paradise Valley Community College addition/renovation brought together 25,956 square feet of student support services into one building to provide one-stop access for all students. Positioned at the center of this rapidly growing campus, the addition transformed the existing introverted mass into an outward reaching, indoor/outdoor environment. It provides access to state-of-the-art facilities within an integrated student/learning environment that fosters collaboration at many levels.

Eight months of collaborative and conceptual planning workshops with the building committee, staff, and students established specific goals and needs for the project that welcomed an open exchange of ideas. The building program consisted of admission and records, counseling and advisement, special services, college safety, gallery commons, student union, student leadership, and a fully renovated student dining facility. Multimedia conference rooms were also constructed for distance learning capabilities.

The project establishes a distinguishable and appropriate presence on campus by embracing the changing physical circumstances around it. It is a facility that projects inward toward campus and presents a welcoming surprise when seen upon entry into the campus. The design represents a collaborative team effort embodying the overall vision of the college.

ARCHITECT
Gould Evans Affiliates

TYPE OF FACILITY
Two-year Technical or Community College

TYPE OF CONSTRUCTION
Addition/Renovation

SITE AREA
1.5 acres

BUILDING AREA
25,916 square feet

TOTAL PROJECT COST
$2,610,255

STATUS OF PROJECT
Completed January 1999

NUMBER OF STUDENTS
7,500

STRUCTURAL ENGINEER
Nabar Stanley Brown

MECHANICAL ENGINEER
Kunka Engineering Inc.

ELECTRICAL ENGINEER
Associated Engineering Inc.

CONTRACTOR
Norquay Construction Inc.

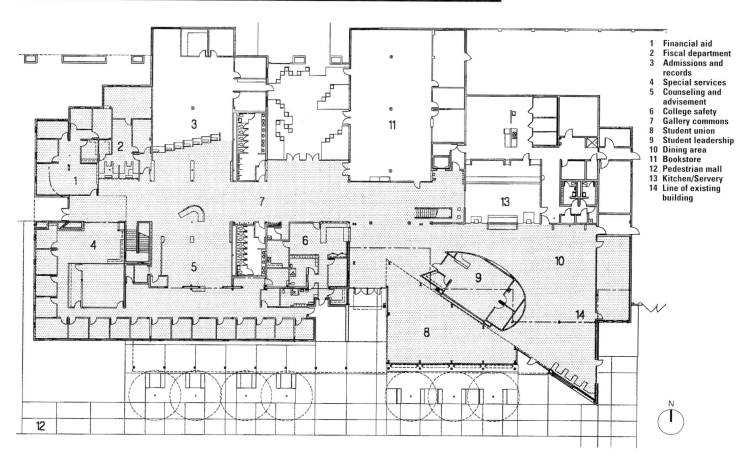

1 Financial aid
2 Fiscal department
3 Admissions and records
4 Special services
5 Counseling and advisement
6 College safety
7 Gallery commons
8 Student union
9 Student leadership
10 Dining area
11 Bookstore
12 Pedestrian mall
13 Kitchen/Servery
14 Line of existing building

UNIQUE LEARNING ENVIRONMENTS

WEAVING THE SCHOOL IN THE CITY

CHARLOTTESVILLE, VIRGINIA

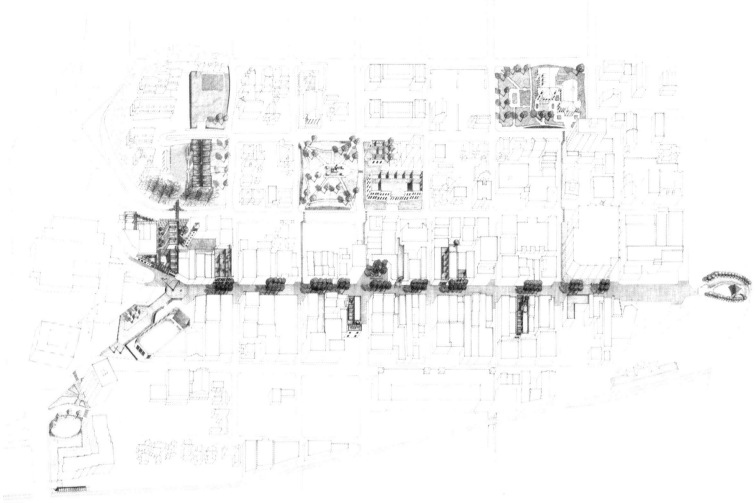

Masterplan

ARCHITECT'S STATEMENT

'Weaving the School in the City' reinvents the traditional educational system as a collection of small schools woven into an urban landscape. The project considers the city as a complex network of spaces which provide a rich learning environment for the students of a K-12 school. Through a process of design, called weaving, classrooms are woven into the voids of the city, connecting the school to the urban community and the students to the world around them.

Using Charlottesville, Virginia, as the test site, the project proposes filling vacant storefront and shop spaces along the Downtown Pedestrian Mall with small 'schools.' The pedestrian mall serves as a connector between the school sites. Along this school path, an elementary school, middle school, and high school are linked to one another as well as to the community

of residents, shops, businesses, and outdoor gathering spaces. The middle school is designated the school center and includes a gathering space that is shared by the schools. The project concludes with a building design problem. The middle school is further developed in order to demonstrate the weaving process at the scale of the school building.

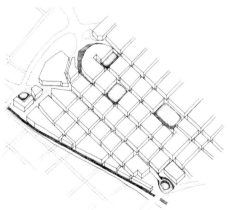

The public space

ARCHITECT
Kerri S. Pleban

TYPE OF FACILITY
Unique Learning Environment

TYPE OF CONSTRUCTION
New/Addition (hypothetical)

SITE AREA
Entire downtown district

BUILDING AREA
Approx. 20,000 square feet per school

NUMBER OF STUDENTS
240 per school

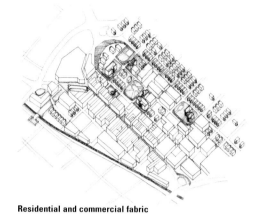

The urban landscape

Residential and commercial fabric

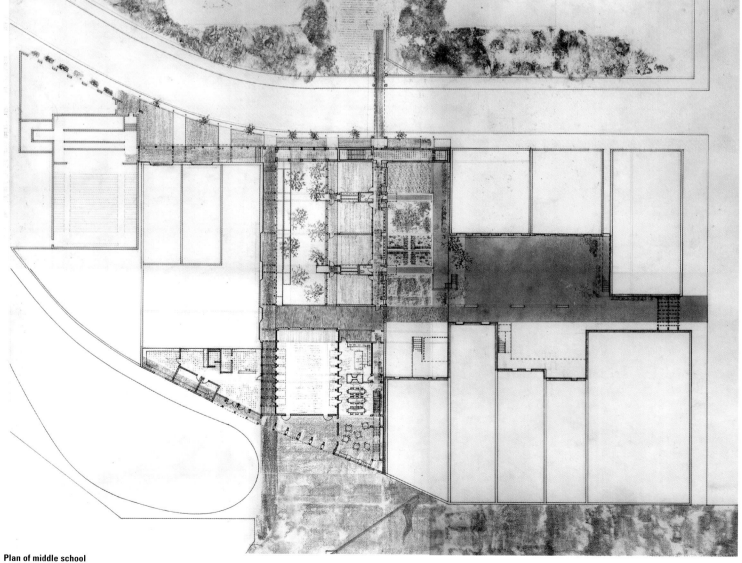

Plan of middle school

DESERT MARIGOLD WALDORF SCHOOL
STRAW-BALE CLASSROOM BUILDING

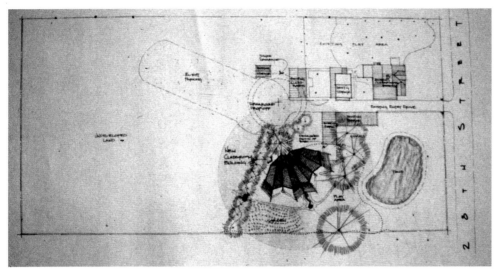

ARCHITECT'S STATEMENT

A diverse community worked together to create a four-classroom kindergarten building and gardens based in Waldorf pedagogy, built with straw-bale construction. This engendered a nurturing place that gently embraces the child and evokes a harmonious connection to its rural surroundings. The community sought to make the building notably environmentally sensitive and energy-efficient, and very respectful of its neighborhood's character.

Finding ways for the school community to fully engage in the design and the construction of the project was especially significant to the design. The hope is the building can be an empowering force for the school and community—through its presence helping to re-energize its languishing neighborhood, and reestablish its living rural nature.

The process has included the community, the builder, and building officials directly in the project, through a series of design and construction workshops and seminars and community-wide design evaluations. Master planning began in Summer 1997, with schematic design in Spring 1998. Fundraising and construction documents were assembled late 1998 through early 1999, construction began in Summer 1999, and opening is planned for Fall 2001.

EXECUTIVE ARCHITECT
Blossom Design Group, Philip Weddle

DESIGN ARCHITECT
Sol Source, Inc., Tom Hahn

TYPE OF FACILITY
Unique Learning Environment / Early Childhood (Kindergarten)

TYPE OF CONSTRUCTION
New

SITE AREA
5.1 acres

BUILDING AREA
3,600 square feet (interior); 5,500 square feet (under roof)

TOTAL PROJECT COST
$280,000 cash/mortgage + approx. $300,000 donated labor/materials

NUMBER OF STUDENTS
64 (180–200 at campus build-out)

STATUS OF PROJECT
Estimated completion Fall 2001

STRUCTURAL ENGINEER
TOR Engineering

MECHANICAL ENGINEER
Otterbein Engineering

ELECTRICAL ENGINEER
Tuley Electrical Design

CONTRACTOR
Wolf Environmental

UNIQUE LEARNING ENVIRONMENTS

THE COLBURN SCHOOL OF PERFORMING ARTS

LOS ANGELES, CALIFORNIA

ARCHITECT'S STATEMENT

The Colburn School of Performing Arts, founded in 1950, was once the preparatory division of the University of Southern California's School of Music. It provides tuition-free music and dance education to nearly 1,000 students, ranging in age from two and a half to 18, and is widely considered one of the finest pre-college music schools in the country.

Until recently, the school was housed in a converted warehouse, where students studied in repetitive rows of dull green cubicles and only two rooms were air-conditioned. Richard Colburn, a major patron and founding member of the board, pledged to fund a new facility when a suitable site could be found.

The new facility is located in the heart of a newly created cultural corridor, recasting the school as a major force in the revitalization of the downtown Los Angeles arts scene. With input from students, faculty, administrators, the school board, and the Community Redevelopment Agency, the resulting design creates a state-of-the-art facility for academic use and professional performances, whose architecture mirrors the dignity, purpose, and importance of the activities inside.

ARCHITECT
**Hardy Holzman Pfeiffer
Associates**

TYPE OF FACILITY
**Alternative School / Unique
Learning Environment**

TYPE OF CONSTRUCTION
New

SITE AREA
2/3 acre

BUILDING AREA
100,000 square feet

TOTAL PROJECT COST
$23 M

STATUS OF PROJECT
Completed October 1998

NUMBER OF STUDENTS
800

STRUCTURAL ENGINEER
John A. Martin & Associates

MECHANICAL/ELECTRICAL/
PLUMBING ENGINEER
Levine/Seegel Associates

CIVIL ENGINEER
Psomas and Associates

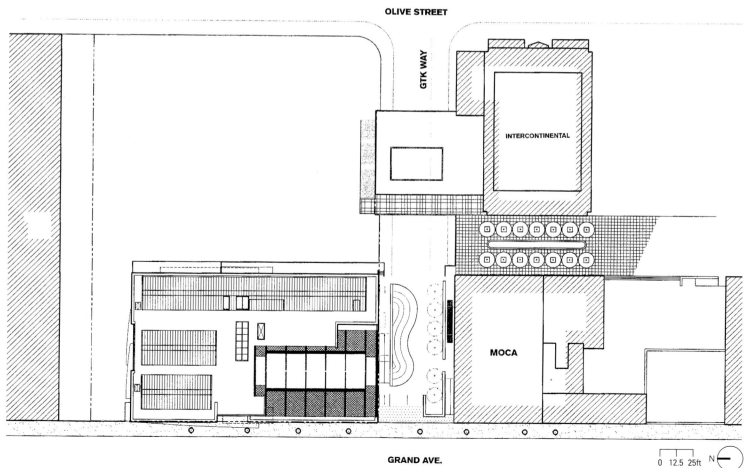

OLIVE STREET

GTK WAY

INTERCONTINENTAL

MOCA

GRAND AVE.

0 12.5 25ft   N

COMMUNITY LEARNING CENTER

CARTERSVILLE, GEORGIA

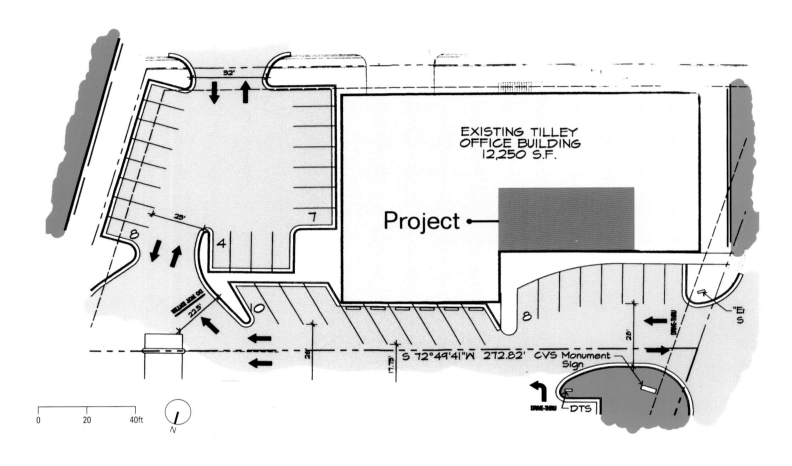

EXISTING TILLEY
OFFICE BUILDING
12,250 S.F.

Project

S 72°49'41"W 272.82' CVS Monument
Sign

DRIVE-THRU   DTS

"E"
S

DRIVE-THRU

0   20   40ft

N

ARCHITECT'S STATEMENT

The project is an adaptive reuse of a historical brick warehouse into a flexible, technology friendly classroom and community learning center.

Under a stringent budget, the goal was to create a multipurpose, flexible space for use as a traditional classroom as well as a technology-based learning environment. We mandated easy integration of technology so that the students or users can operate in a networked PC or laptop environment. We also wanted to incorporate and preserve time-tested aspects of classroom learning and group interaction environments. The goal was to avoid the static, hardwired settings that dominate today's media labs or learning centers.

The design solution centered around a densely pre-wired power and data network embedded beneath a low profile floor to create a flexible, plug and play 'smart environment.' Cabling is concealed but connections are easily accessible allowing for a myriad of configurations and multiple learning activities. Preservation of the brick walls and ceiling structures was also achieved by not having to run conduit or wire moldings. Local businesses and schools participated in the project.

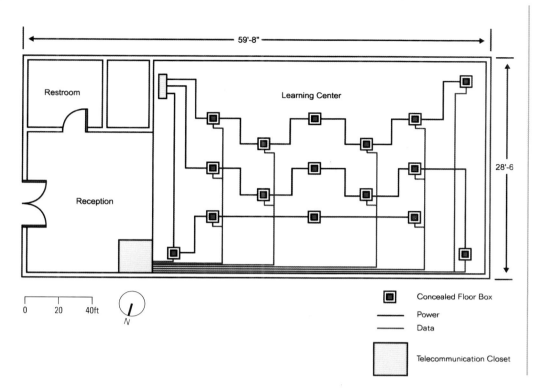

ARCHITECT
Connect Center Inc.

CONTRACTOR
Custom Builders (Interior Construction)

TYPE OF FACILITY
High School / Innovative Learning Environment / Corporate or Other Specialized Training Center / Other or Multipurpose / Unique Learning Environment

TYPE OF CONSTRUCTION
Renovation

NUMBER OF STUDENTS
40

BUILDING AREA
12,250 square feet

TOTAL PROJECT COST
$50 M

STATUS OF PROJECT
Completion March 1999

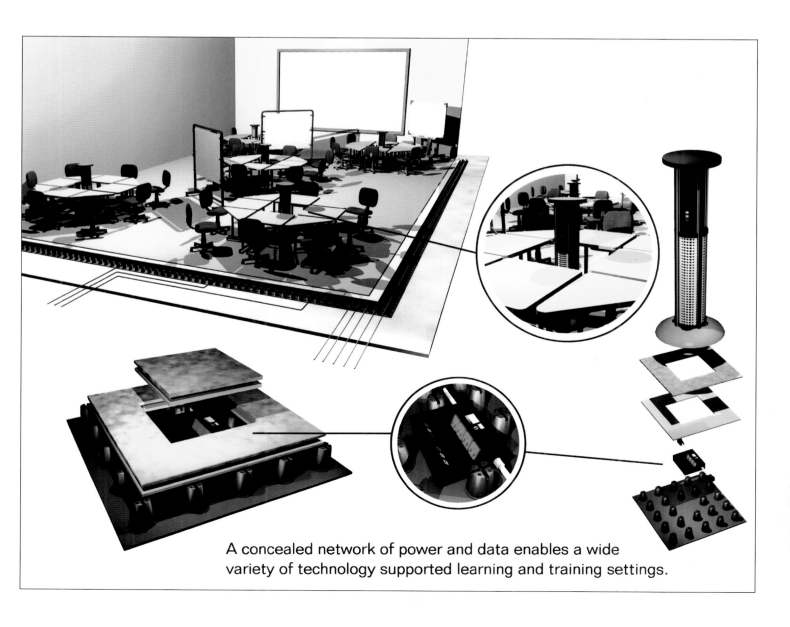

A concealed network of power and data enables a wide variety of technology supported learning and training settings.

LEAKE & WATTS SCHOOL AND HOME

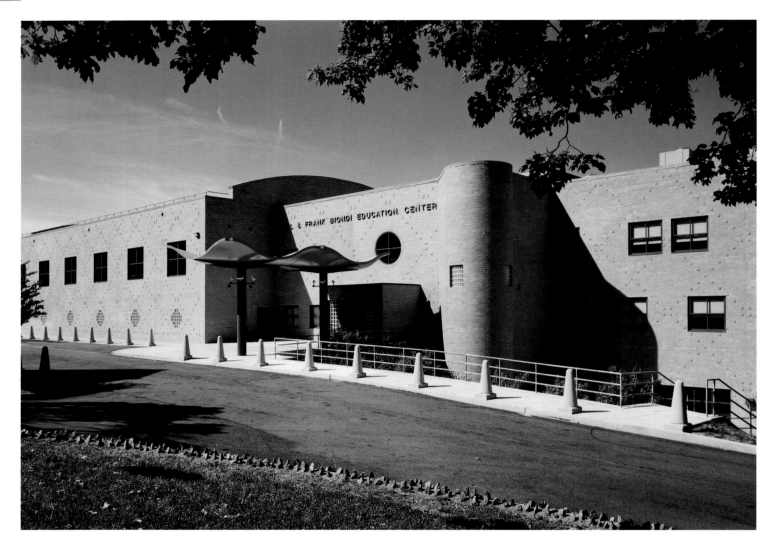

ARCHITECT'S STATEMENT

Leake and Watts Services, Inc. has served New York City's children and families in need since its founding in 1831. In the early 1990s, the agency embarked on a capital project at its main campus, a tree-filled 30 acre site overlooking the Hudson River designed in 1898 by Frederick Law Olmsted. Our project was completed in 1998.

Campus facilities house and school emotionally disturbed teenagers from troubled homes. The agency's goal is to enable these children to gain self-respect, security, social responsibility, and vocational skills during their residence.

The design process began with the designers living with residents for two days, joining meals, household chores, recreation, and school. We also interviewed agency staff and administrators. These activities led to a design comprising a series of 'worlds' of increasing socialization and responsibility delineated within nine new residential cottages grouped into three villages each with a shared village green and a 'care cottage.' Two rehabilitated cottages, the new 200-pupil Biondi Educational Center, and the renovation of the original building complete the work designed by our firm. The functional core of the Leake & Watts community is the new Educational Center tucked into a hillside and serving both residents and pupils with special needs from the surrounding community. The curved façades mimic natural site contours, soften the impact of the new building, and allow most classrooms to face the river. A central spine divides the school into a north wing—containing classrooms, laboratories and shops, library, offices, and a dining facility, and a south wing—housing the gymnasium, swimming pool, lockers, student center, and multipurpose auditorium. These social and sports spaces function independently after school hours, and are available for community use.

ARCHITECT
Richard Dattner Architect, P.C.

TYPE OF FACILITY
Early Childhood Learning Environment / High School / Other or Multipurpose / Unique Learning Environment

TYPE OF CONSTRUCTION
New

SITE AREA
30.5 acres

BUILDING AREA
146,316 square feet

TOTAL PROJECT COST
$15,380,000

STATUS OF PROJECT
Residential completed 1995; School completed 1998

NUMBER OF STUDENTS
200

STRUCTURAL ENGINEER
Ysrael A. Seinuk, P.C.

MECHANICAL/ELECTRICAL ENGINEER
Mariano D. Molina, P.C.

CONTRACTOR
Andron Construction Corp.

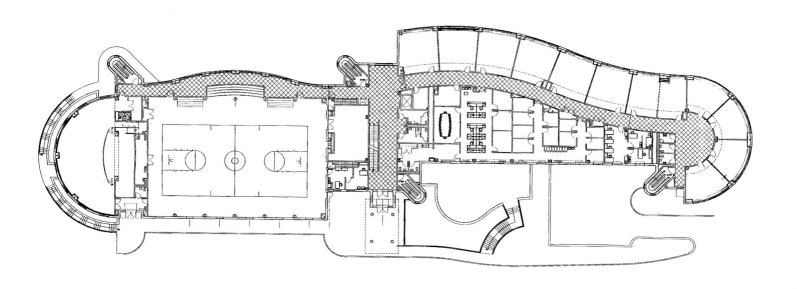

SCHOOL FOR THE ILLINOIS INSTITUTE OF TECHNOLOGY COMMUNITY CHILDREN

Academic part

- public zone
- flexible space
- open to the spine
- anchored by 2 pavilions

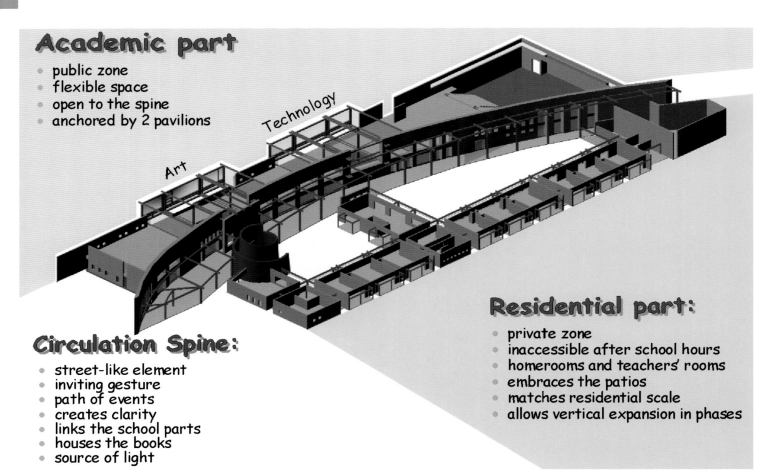

Technology

Art

Circulation Spine:

- street-like element
- inviting gesture
- path of events
- creates clarity
- links the school parts
- houses the books
- source of light

Residential part:

- private zone
- inaccessible after school hours
- homerooms and teachers' rooms
- embraces the patios
- matches residential scale
- allows vertical expansion in phases

ARCHITECT'S STATEMENT

The aim of this thesis was to design a school, as part of the long-term master plan for the Illinois Institute of Technology (IIT) to accommodate preschool through eighth grade, and serve the growing community after school hours. The challenge was to create an inviting and stimulating environment with its own spirit reinforcing children's sense of belonging, and to integrate it within the unique Mies Van der Rohe campus. Better understanding of children's special needs was gained through direct interaction with Crow Island elementary school students. Following the concept of 'campus inside a campus,' the clarity in use was gained by dividing the school into the academic and residential parts, similar to the IIT campus. The two parts are connected by an inviting

street-like spine that serves both learning and social purposes. The unique feature of the design is the implementation of a concept of 'the school as a library.' To reinforce the role of the books as an important educational resource, the books were made visible and accessible by extending the library into the spine.

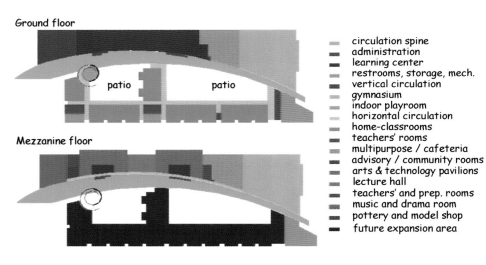

Ground floor

patio   patio

Mezzanine floor

- circulation spine
- administration
- learning center
- restrooms, storage, mech.
- vertical circulation
- gymnasium
- indoor playroom
- horizontal circulation
- home-classrooms
- teachers' rooms
- multipurpose / cafeteria
- advisory / community rooms
- arts & technology pavilions
- lecture hall
- teachers' and prep. rooms
- music and drama room
- pottery and model shop
- future expansion area

ARCHITECT
Anat Mor-Avi

TYPE OF FACILITY
**Early Childhood Learning
Environment / Elementary /
Middle/Junior High School /
Unique Learning Environment**

TYPE OF CONSTRUCTION
**Thesis
(Advisor: Susan Conger-Austin)**

NUMBER OF STUDENTS
250–500

BUILDING AREA
80,000 square feet

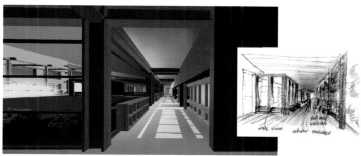

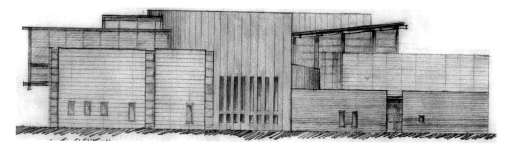

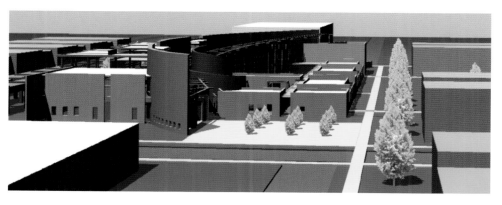

EDUCATIONAL FACILITIES

OTHER OR MULTIPURPOSE

GREAT SWAMP ENVIRONMENTAL SCIENCE CENTER
CITATION

ARCHITECT'S STATEMENT

The Great Swamp Environmental Science Center is the culmination of more than 30 years' conservation effort focused on preserving the Great Swamp and its tributary watershed.

A unique environmental education center devoted to public education, the Science Center was born amid the realization that the long-term health of this federally designated wildlife refuge, located in the New York metropolitan-north central New Jersey area, could only be assured by public education and public awareness. Denigrated water quality from surrounding communities is the largest single threat to the long-term health of the Great Swamp.

Programs will highlight the impacts on the larger watershed created by individual acts, development pressure, and misplaced public policy.

The Great Swamp Science Center will inform and educate on all of these levels and will, in conjunction with an area-wide system of information kiosks and directions, foster a regional awareness of environmental quality.

Programmatically the Science Center project consists of four principal elements:

Botanical Shed structure: housing the four principal ecologies found within this particular watershed from wooded uplands to freshwater marsh, the structure consists of large timber frames encased in a glass and metal skin. The Botanical Shed portrays a reclaimed 19th century agricultural building or barn, and includes random dry-laid stone walls and a stone and cinder floor. It is complemented at the north and south end of the complex by companion structures simulating small out buildings when viewed from the upland end of the site.

Science Center structure: the glass pyramid of the Science Center emerges from the Botanical Shed at the crest of the Great Swamp marshes. It is a simple and pristine shape and contains within it a suspended galley way over a full topographic depiction of the complete watershed, representing a 70 square mile area. Outlooks and walkouts provide direct views to the open wetlands beyond the complex. The structure is non-intrusive through its simplicity of form and material.

Various scenarios will be portrayed utilizing the watershed model and illustrating past and potential impacts on the refuge and its surrounding area.

Development models will range from the prehistoric, pre-colonial, colonial/ agricultural to the industrial eras of the more recent past. Special emphasis will be directed toward varying models of future impacts by mapping the various choices for

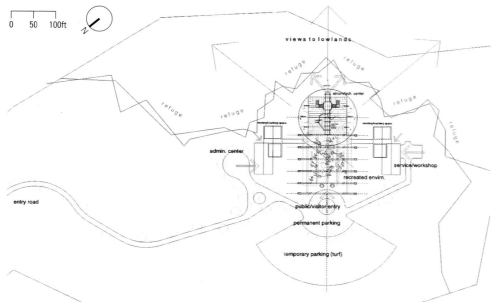

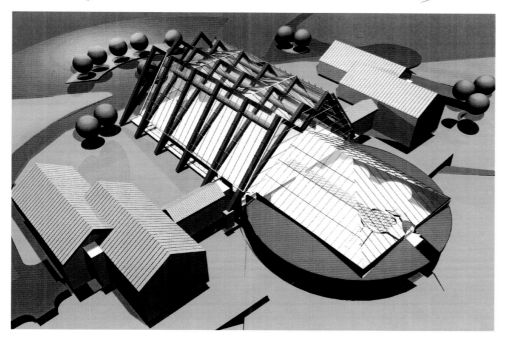

ARCHITECT
Kimmerle Architects

TYPE OF FACILITY
Other or Multipurpose

TYPE OF CONSTRUCTION
New

NUMBER OF STUDENTS
100,000

SITE AREA
7 acres

BUILDING AREA
30,000 square feet

TOTAL PROJECT COST
$175/square foot (estimate)

future development of the watershed. The impact of individual, zoning, and public proposals will depict ranges from rampant growth to preservation via land conservation and trust acquisitions.

Surrounding the watershed model is a series of exhibits/displays each providing exposure to individual environmental demonstrations. A team of volunteer docents will lead visitors in either hands-on experiments or discussion sessions on a series of topics concerning the watershed and each individual's role in its preservation.

Laboratory/Research Building: the southern outbuilding contains research and laboratory facilities for student and educator study in environmental sciences. This facility will function as an annex within the refuge for area colleges and universities.

Administrative/Resource Building: the northern outbuilding contains general administrative offices, lecture and training rooms as well as the conservancy's resource library. It will serve as the site of ongoing public meetings, presentations, and consortium.

The center will also maintain an Internet site linking area libraries and local municipal offices to the wealth of environmental studies developed by the sponsors over the past 30 years.

It is believed that this resource, in conjunction with a wider public awareness of criteria important to refuge/watershed welfare, will inform local decision making in the interest of the long-term betterment of not only the Great Swamp but the quality of life for the community at large.

HORIZONTE INSTRUCTION AND TRAINING CENTER

SALT LAKE CITY, UTAH

ARCHITECT'S STATEMENT

Salt Lake Community High School started 20 years ago as an alternative high school for students not conforming to the standard K-12 curriculum. At the time this was a new concept implemented by principal James Anderson to rescue dropouts and kids with behavioral problems who had been expelled. Over the years, adult education programs were added, including English as a second language. The school became the place for those students that educators and the community did not want to be bothered with—a population of dysfunctional, hard-to-teach, or non-English speaking people. The school was housed in an abandoned junior high school, out of site, out of mind.

In 1993 a bond was passed to seismically upgrade all city schools. Salt Lake Community High School was needed as a transition facility while one of the high

schools was retrofitted, then scheduled for demolition. A new site was needed for the school. From that, Horizonte Instruction and Training Center was designed with the following mission:

To value the diversity and individual worth of students. To be a multicultural learning center. To provide the education and skills necessary for students to achieve self-sufficiency and become contributing participants in their communities. To create an atmosphere that encourages educating the individual now and throughout life-long learning.

The center accommodates approximately 1,200 students in the new building. However, it actually services over 9,300 students around the city. High schoolers and a variety of adult learners—ESL, basic education, political refugees, new

immigrants, unwed parents, and students not able to make it in the mainstream educational system—learn in this new facility. The facility is linked to over 50 different public, private, and non-profit organizations by computer to help reach those unable to attend class in the building.

Students will eventually be 100 percent 'linked' via computer in the new school. Every teacher will give out assignments by computer, students will complete the work and submit back to the teacher by computer. Grades, exams, all aspects of the educational process will be conducted by computer, making Horizonte a truly paperless school.

ARCHITECT
Valentiner Crane Brunjes Onyon Architects

TYPE OF FACILITY
Alternative School / Innovative Learning Environment / Two-year Technical or Community College / Corporate or Other Specialized Training Center / Other or Multipurpose

TYPE OF CONSTRUCTION
New

NUMBER OF STUDENTS
1,200

BUILDING AREA
110,000 square feet

TOTAL PROJECT COST
$10,750,00

STATUS OF PROJECT
Completed July 1996

STRUCTURAL ENGINEER
Reaveley Engineering

MECHANICAL ENGINEER
Van Boerum & Frank

ELECTRICAL ENGINEER
BNA Consulting Engineers II

CONTRACTOR
Oakland Constructions

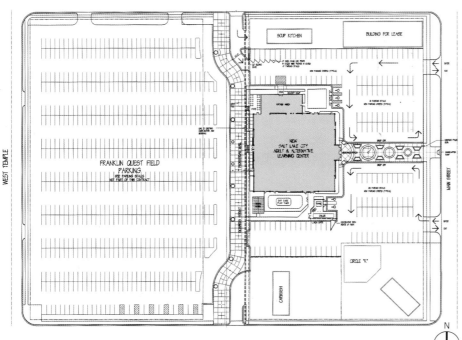

OTHER OR MULTIPURPOSE

PHOTOGRAPHIC CREDITS

Adam Joseph Lewis Center for Environmental Studies
Photography: William McDonough + Partners, pp. 152, 153

Alpha High School
Photography: Uwe Schneider, pp. 146, 147

The Althea Gibson Early Childhood Education Academy
Photography: James D'Addio, pp. 16, 17

Benjamin Franklin Elementary School
Photography: Robert Benson, pp. 42, 43

Berkeley High School, Buildings G and H
Photography: Michael Bruk, pp. 106, 107

Brewster Academy Classroom/Library Expansion
Photography: John Horner, pp. 108, 109

Brownsburg Challenger Learning Center
Photography: Garry Chilluffo (interior); John Fleck (exterior), pp. 164, 165

Building Blocks Montessori School at The Learning Corridor
Photography: Gilbane Building Company (aerial photograph); Robert Benson
Photography, pp. 166, 167

Carmel High School
Photography: Timothy Hursley, pp. 100, 111

Centennial Academic and Arts Center, Pomfret School
Photography: Steve Rosenthal, pp. 112, 113

Centennial Campus Magnet Middle School
Photography: Steve Rosenthal, pp. 80, 81

Center for Interactive Learning
Photography: Hedrich Blessing (interior); J. Miles Wolf (exterior),
pp. 194, 195

Centre de formation professionnelle électrotechnique et machine fixe
Photography: Video Delta, pp. 196, 197

Cesar Chavez Elementary School
Photography: Jim Brady, pp. 36, 37

Children's Center Campus
Photography: Mike Sinclair, pp. 170, 171

Claire Lilienthal Elementary School
Photography: Donna Kempner, pp. 44, 45

Dakota High School
Photography: Emery Photography, Inc., pp. 114, 115

Dakota Ridge High School
Photography: Thorney Lieberman, pp. 116, 117

Day Care Inc.
Photography: Michael Dersin, pp. 18, 19

Decker Health Sciences Building
Photography: Jon Reis, pp. 198, 199

Derby Middle School
Photography: Gary Quesada, Hedrich Blessing, pp. 82, 83

Desert Marigold Waldorf School Straw-bale Classroom Building
Photography: Tom Hahn, pp. 212, 213

Des Moines Area Community College—Newton Polytechnic Campus
Photography: Dale Photographics Inc., pp. 200, 201

Discovery Middle School
Photography: Ed Vidinghoff, pp. 74, 75

Donald A. Quarles Elementary School
Photography: B&H Photographics, pp. 20, 21

Early Education Center
Photography: Peter Vanderwarker (interior); Anton Grassl (exterior),
pp. 22, 23

EarthWorks
Photography: Mike Sinclair, pp. 154, 155

East Valley Institute of Technology
Photography: Walt Saadus and William Timmerman, pp. 172, 173

Edmonds-Woodway High School
Photography: James F. Housel, pp. 118, 119

Francis Child Development Institute, Penn Valley Community College
Photography: Mike Sinclair, pp. 24, 25

Genko Uchida Building
Photography: Greg Premru, pp. 174, 175

Glendale Campus, Niagara College Canada
Photography: Kerun Ip, pp. 202, 203

Glendale Community College Applied Sciences Teaching Lab
Photography: Bill Timmerman, pp. 204, 205

Grainger Center for Imagination and Inquiry
Photography: Scott McDonald, Hedrich Blessing, pp. 156, 157

Grandview High School
Photography: Jim Berchert, pp. 120, 121

Gretchko Elementary School
Photography: Gary Quesada, Hedrich Blessing, pp. 26, 27

Haggerty School
Photography: Nick Wheeler Photographics, pp. 46, 47

Harford Glen Environmental Education Center
Photography: Michael Campbell, pp. 176, 177

Horace Mann School
Photography: Jock Pottle/Esto Photographics (model photography);
Lenon Models (site/building model), pp. 76, 77

Horizonte Instruction and Training Center
Photography: Scot Zimmerman Photography, pp. 226, 227

James Madison School of Excellence
Photography: Tim Wilkes (interior/exterior); James Cavanaugh (models/site
plans), pp. 84, 85

James F. Oyster Elementary School
Photography: Rendered images created by Jacobs Facilities Inc., pp. 48, 49

Juan Rodriguez Cabrillo High School
Photography: Milroy & AcAleer, pp. 122, 123

Kapolei Middle School
Photography: Steven D. Wong, pp. 86, 87

Kent Island High School
Photography: Kenneth M. Wyner; Dan Cunningham, pp. 104, 105

KidPower/New York Hall of Science Playground
Photography: Peter Mauss/Esto Photographics, pp. 158, 159

King Urban Life Center and King Center Charter School
Photography: Biff Henrich; Charles Massey, pp. 14, 15

Lake Orion High School
Photography: Gary Quesada/Hedrich Blessing, pp. 124, 125

LakeView Technology Academy
Photography: Robert Sabonjian, pp. 178, 179

Leake & Watts School and Home
Photography: Peter Mauss/Esto Photographics, pp. 218, 219

Lick-Wilmerding Library/Arts & Humanities Building
Photography: Timothy Hursley (image 1 & 2 bottom left), p. 126;
Richard Barnes (image 3, bottom right), p. 127

Long Beach International Elementary School
Photography: Tom Bonner, pp. 32, 33

Longmeadow Center Elementary School
Photography: Steve Rosenthal, pp. 50, 51

Manassas Park High School
Photography: Chris Barrett, Hedrich Blessing; Jackson Smith, pp. 102, 103

Manhattan Village Academy High School
Photography: Peter Aaron/Esto Photographics, pp. 128, 129

Meredith Hill Elementary School
Photography: Steve Keating Photography, pp. 52, 53

Meysen Academy, Kamiyagari Campus
Photography: Art Grise, pp. 180, 181

Miami Edison Middle School
Photography: Dan Forer, Photographer, pp. 88, 89

Morgan Hill Country School
Photography: Bonnie Bridges, pp. 54, 55

Moylan Elementary School
Photography: Timothy Hursley, pp. 56, 57

Neal Smith National Wildlife Refuge Prairie Learning Center
Photography: Thorney Lieberman, pp. 182, 183

Nelda Mundy Elementary School
Photography: Michael Bruk, pp. 58, 59

New Magnet Program—Center for Pre-Law & Legal Studies
Photography: E. "Manny" Abraben, AIA, Arch. Photography, Inc.,
pp. 130, 131

New Southwest High School
Photography: Gary Quesada, Hedrich Blessing, pp. 132, 133

New Technology High School
Photography: Technical Imagery Studios of Santa Rosa, California,
pp. 134, 135

Oxford Hills Comprehensive High School
Photography: Greg Morley, pp. 136, 137

P.S. 56/The Louis DeSario Elementary School
Photography: Jeff Goldberg/Esto Photographics, pp. 62, 63

Pleasant Ridge Middle School
Photography: Mike Sinclair, pp. 90, 91

Rancho Del Rey Middle School
Photography: Jim Brady, pp. 92, 93

Rusk Children's Playgarden for Interactive Therapeutic Play
Photography: Sonja Johansson (image 1), p. 160; Stephanie Molen (image 1),
p. 161; Playground Environments International, Inc. pp. 160, 161; Thomas
Schaller (rendering), p. 161; JDC Inc. (formerly Johansson & Walcavage)
(plan), p. 161

Salisbury School
Photography: David Franzen, pp. 162, 163

Saltonstall Elementary School
Photography: Nick Wheeler, pp. 64, 65

School for the Physical City
Photography: Roy J. Wright, pp. 148, 149

Shoreline Early Education Center
Photography: Robert Dittmer, pp. 28, 29

Star Valley High School
Photography: Scot Zimmerman Photography, pp. 140, 141

Student Support Services, Paradise Valley Community College
Photography: Bill Timmerman Photography, pp. 206, 207

Tenderloin Community School
Photography: Ethan Kaplan (front façade), p. 34; Mark Darley (small
classroom), p. 34; EHDD (exterior trellis), p. 35

The Colburn School of Performing Arts
Photography: Foaad Farah, pp. 214, 215

Timbercrest Junior High School
Photography: Land.Image (lower left), p. 95; Northwest Architectural
Company, pp. 94, 95

Travis L. Williams Family Services Center
Photography: Landiscor (aerial photography); Linda Enger (portrait
photography), pp. 184, 185

Veterans Park Schools
Photography: Renderings by Wallace H. McTammany, pp. 96, 97

Walnut Hills Arts & Science Center
Photography: J. Miles Wolf, pp. 186, 187

Waverly High School
Photography: Tom Kessler of Kessler Photography, pp. 142, 143

Weaving a School into the City
Renderings/plans: Kerri S. Pleban, pp. 210, 211

Whittier Community School for the Arts
Photography: Don F. Wong, pp. 66, 67

Whittier Elementary School
Photography: Chris J. Roberts, pp. 68, 69

Wilbert Snow Elementary School
Photography: Woodruff/Brown, pp. 40, 41

Windsor Middle School
Photography: Technical Imagery Studios of Santa Rosa, California, pp. 98, 99

Wisdom Hall, Antioch Community High School District 117
Photography: Christopher Barrett, Hedrich Blessing, pp. 188, 189

Wycallis Elementary
Photography: Jeff Goldberg/Esto Photographics, pp. 70, 71

ACKNOWLEDGMENTS

IMAGES is pleased to add *Educational Facilities: The American Institute of Architects Exemplary Learning Environment Program* to its compendium of design and architectural publications.

We wish to thank all participating firms for their valuable contribution to this publication.